LONDON
GUIDE 2023

A BEGINNER'S GUIDE TO EXPLORING THE CITY LIKE A PRO

Olivia Falorn

COPYRIGHT

TABLE OF CONTENT

INTRODUCTION

Welcome to "London Travel Guide 2023: A Beginner's Guide to Exploring the City Like a Pro"!

If you're planning a trip to London, chances are you're feeling a mix of excitement and nerves. London is a city that has something for everyone - from the iconic Big Ben and Tower Bridge to the winding alleys of Covent Garden and the fashionable boutiques of Oxford Street - but with so much to see and do, it can be overwhelming for first-time visitors to know where to start.

That's where this book comes in. "London Travel Guide 2023" is designed to be your ultimate guide to exploring the city, whether you're interested in art and history, shopping and dining, or simply soaking up the city's vibrant atmosphere. In these pages, you'll find a wealth of information on the city's top attractions, as well as insider tips and tricks on how to make the most of your time in London.

But "London Travel Guide 2023" isn't just a guide to the city's top attractions. We'll also take you on a tour of some of the city's lesser-known neighborhoods and introduce you to some of the locals who call London home. We'll give you practical advice on how to get around the city, from navigating the underground subway system to hailing a classic black cab. And we'll recommend some of the best restaurants, pubs, and markets to visit, as well as some local specialties to try.

So whether you're a first-time visitor to London or a seasoned traveler looking to discover something new, "London Travel Guide 2023" has something for you. Grab your map, pack your bags, and get ready to explore the city like a pro!

Now, let's dive in and get to know London a little better.

London is a city that has something for everyone, and it's no surprise that it's one of the most visited cities in the world. From the towering heights of the London Eye to the peaceful green spaces of Hyde Park, the city is full of iconic landmarks that draw millions of visitors each year.

But London is so much more than just its landmarks. It's a city with a rich history and culture, with roots that date back to the ancient Roman Empire. The city's streets are lined with historic buildings and monuments, from the majestic Buckingham Palace to the iconic Tower of London.

And of course, no trip to London is complete without sampling the city's world-renowned cuisine. From classic British pub food to the latest foodie trends, London has something for every taste and budget. You'll find some of the best restaurants, pubs, and markets in the city, as well as local specialties like fish and chips and afternoon tea.

But London isn't just a city for tourists - it's also home to millions of locals who know the city like the back of their hand. In "London

Travel Guide 2023", we'll introduce you to some of the city's best neighborhoods and give you the scoop on what it's really like to live in the city. From the trendy neighborhoods of Shoreditch and Notting Hill to the historic charm of Kensington and Chelsea, there's something for everyone in London.

So whether you're interested in art and history, shopping and dining, or simply soaking up the city's vibrant atmosphere, "London Travel Guide 2023" has something for you. We'll guide you through the city's top attractions and give you the insider tips and tricks you need to make the most of your trip.

And of course, we'll give you practical advice on how to get around the city, from navigating the underground subway system to hailing a classic black cab. We'll recommend some of the best neighborhoods to explore and introduce you to some of the locals who call London home.

But "London Travel Guide 2023" isn't just a guide to the city's top attractions and neighborhoods - it's also a resource for anyone looking to make the most of their trip to the city. We'll give you practical advice on how to plan your trip, from finding the best flights and accommodations to budgeting for your trip.

And once you arrive in London, we'll give you tips on how to make the most of your time in the city. We'll recommend some of the best activities and experiences, from touring the city's iconic landmarks to taking a leisurely stroll through one of the city's many parks. We'll also give you the inside scoop on some of the city's best-kept secrets, from hidden rooftop bars to underground clubs and live music venues.

So whether you're a first-time visitor to London or a seasoned traveler looking to discover something new, "London Travel Guide 2023" has something for you. With our comprehensive guide, you'll have everything you need to make the most of your trip to this incredible city. So grab your map, pack your bags, and get ready to explore London like a pro!

CHAPTER 1

WELCOME TO LONDON!

Welcome to London, a beautiful and vibrant city that is sure to captivate you with its rich history, cultural diversity, and iconic landmarks. From the towering heights of Big Ben and the London Eye, to the bustling streets of Oxford Circus and the iconic red telephone boxes, there is something for everyone to enjoy in London. Whether you are visiting for the first time or returning for another adventure, you will find a wealth of things to see and do in this exciting city.

History and Culture of London

London is the capital and largest city of England and the United Kingdom. It is a diverse and vibrant city with a rich history and culture that dates back thousands of years.

The history of London begins with the Romans, who founded the city in AD 43. They called it Londinium and it became an important center for trade and commerce. The Romans built roads, aqueducts, and walls around the city to protect it from invaders.

After the fall of the Roman Empire, London continued to thrive as a center of trade and commerce. It became an important port and was home to many merchants and artisans. The city also played a significant role in the development of the English language, which evolved from a mixture of Latin, Old English, and other languages spoken by the people who lived in the city.

Throughout its history, London has been a center of political power and influence. It has been the capital of England since the 12th century and has played a central role in the development of the British Empire and the United Kingdom. Many important political events have taken place in the city, including the signing of the Magna Carta in 1215 and the founding of the London Stock Exchange in the 17th century.

London has a long and varied literary history. It was home to many famous writers, including William Shakespeare, Charles Dickens, and Oscar Wilde. The city has also been the setting for many classic works of literature, such as "Oliver Twist" and "Great Expectations."

The city's music scene is diverse and vibrant, with a variety of genres represented. London has been home to many famous musicians, including The Rolling Stones, The Beatles, and Adele. The city is also home to the Royal Opera House and the Royal Albert Hall, two of the most prestigious music venues in the world.

London is home to a wide variety of sporting events and activities. It has hosted the Olympic Games twice, in 1908 and 2012, and is home to many professional sports teams, including football (soccer) clubs such as Arsenal and Chelsea, and rugby clubs such as Saracens and Harlequins.

The city's food and drink culture is diverse and influential. London is home to many Michelin-starred restaurants and has a thriving street food scene. It is also home to a number of famous pubs, such as The Churchill Arms and The George Inn.

London has a long and storied history of cultural and artistic expression. The city has been home to many famous artists and writers, including William Blake, J.M.W. Turner, and Virginia Woolf. It is also home to a number of world-renowned galleries and museums, such as the National Gallery and the Victoria and Albert Museum.

The city is known for its vibrant theater scene, with numerous theaters showcasing a range of performances, from classic plays and musicals to cutting-edge experimental works. The West End is home to many of the city's most famous theaters, including the Royal Opera House and the London Palladium.

London is also home to a number of important cultural festivals, including the Notting Hill Carnival, which is the largest street festival in Europe, and the Pride in London parade, which celebrates the city's LGBTQ+ community.

The city is home to a number of iconic landmarks, such as Big Ben and the Houses of Parliament, the Tower Bridge, and St. Paul's Cathedral. These landmarks are popular tourist attractions and are often used as symbols of London and the United Kingdom.

London has a diverse and multicultural population, with more than 300 languages spoken in the city. This diversity is reflected in the city's many neighborhoods, each with its own unique character and culture.

Throughout its history, London has been home to many different cultures and communities. It has a long tradition of welcoming immigrants from around the world, which has contributed to its rich cultural diversity. This diversity is reflected in the city's many neighborhoods, each with its own unique character and history.

London is also home to many world-famous landmarks and cultural institutions, such as Buckingham Palace, the Tower of London, the British Museum, and the Tate Modern. These attractions draw millions of visitors each year and are a testament to the city's rich history and cultural significance.

In addition to its history and cultural institutions, London is also known for its diverse and vibrant arts and entertainment scene. The city is home to numerous theaters, galleries, and music venues, as well as a thriving food and drink culture.

In conclusion, London is a city with a rich and diverse history and culture that has shaped the city into the vibrant and cosmopolitan place it is today. Its many landmarks, cultural institutions, and diverse communities all contribute to its unique character and make it a must-visit destination for anyone interested in history and culture.

Top 15 Reasons London is a Must-See
Here are the top 15 reasons you should visit London:

❖ **Rich history and culture**

London is a city with a rich and varied history, with a number of world-renowned landmarks and cultural institutions. The city has been a center of political power and influence for centuries and has played a central role in the development of the British Empire and the United Kingdom. London is also home to many famous artists and writers, such as William Shakespeare and Charles Dickens, and has a number of world-class galleries and museums, such as the National Gallery and the Victoria and Albert Museum.

❖ **Landmarks and attractions**

London is home to many iconic landmarks and attractions, such as Buckingham Palace, the Tower of London, the British Museum, and the Tate Modern. These landmarks and attractions are popular tourist destinations and are a testament to the city's rich history and cultural significance.

❖ **Diverse neighborhoods**

Each of London's neighborhoods has its own unique character and culture, making it a great city to explore. From the trendy neighborhoods of Shoreditch and Notting Hill to the historic neighborhoods of Westminster and the City of London, there is something for everyone in this diverse city.

❖ **Vibrant arts and entertainment scene**

London has a thriving arts and entertainment scene, with numerous theaters, galleries, and music venues. The city is home to a number of world-class theaters, such as the Royal Opera House and the London Palladium, and is a center for contemporary art, with galleries such as the Tate Modern and the Saatchi Gallery.

❖ **World-class shopping**

London is a shopper's paradise, with a wide variety of high-end retailers, markets, and department stores. From luxury brands on Bond Street to vintage clothing at Camden Market, there is something for everyone in the city's many shopping districts.

❖ **Delicious food and drink**

London has a diverse and dynamic food and drink culture, with a range of Michelin-starred restaurants and a thriving street food scene. The city is also home to a number of famous pubs, such as The Churchill Arms and The George Inn, and is known for its excellent tea and coffee culture.

❖ **Excellent transportation**

London has an efficient and comprehensive transportation system, making it easy to get around the city. The city has an extensive network of buses, trains, and underground trains (the "Tube"), as well as a number of bike-sharing and ride-sharing options.

❖ **Beautiful parks and green spaces**

London is home to a number of beautiful parks and green spaces, such as Hyde Park and Regent's Park. These parks are popular destinations for picnics, outdoor sports, and relaxation, and offer a respite from the hustle and bustle of the city.

❖ **Sports and outdoor activities**

London is home to a number of professional sports teams, including football (soccer) clubs such as Arsenal and Chelsea, and rugby clubs such as Saracens and Harlequins. The city also has a number of outdoor activities to enjoy, such as cycling and boating on the Thames.

❖ **World-class universities**

London is home to a number of prestigious universities, making it a great place for education and research. The city is home to institutions such as the University of Oxford and the University of Cambridge, as well as a number of other top-ranked universities.

❖ **Diverse and multicultural population**

London is home to a diverse and multicultural population, with over 300 languages spoken in the city. This diversity is reflected in the city's many neighborhoods, each with its own unique character and culture.

❖ Excellent healthcare

London has a world-class healthcare system, making it a safe and reliable place to visit. The city has a number of top-ranked hospitals and is home to a number of leading medical research institutions.

❖ Dynamic business and financial center

London is a global business and financial center, with a number of important financial institutions and corporate headquarters. The city is home to the London Stock Exchange and the Bank of England, as well as a number of other major financial institutions.

❖ Great weather

London has a temperate climate, with mild winters and cool summers. This makes it a great destination year-round, with plenty of outdoor activities to enjoy in the milder months and a variety of indoor attractions to explore during the colder months.

❖ Easy to reach from anywhere

London is easily accessible from anywhere in the world, with a number of international airports and excellent transportation links. The city is well-connected by air, rail, and road, making it easy to get to from anywhere in the world.

Geography and Neighborhoods

The city is located on the River Thames and is divided into 32 boroughs, each with its own local government.

The geography of London is varied, with a number of different landscapes within the city limits. The city is home to a number of green spaces, including Hyde Park and Regent's Park, as well as a number of canals and rivers, such as the Thames and the Regent's Canal. London is also home to a number of hills, including Hampstead Heath and Primrose Hill, which offer views of the city.

London is a large and diverse city, with a number of distinct neighborhoods, each with its own character and culture. Some of the city's most famous neighborhoods include:

❖ **The City of London**

The City of London is the historic center of the city and is home to a number of financial institutions and corporate headquarters. It is also home to a number of historic landmarks, such as St. Paul's Cathedral and the Tower of London.

❖ **Westminster**

Westminster is home to many of the city's most famous landmarks, such as Buckingham Palace and the Houses of Parliament. It is a busy and vibrant neighborhood, with a number of shops, restaurants, and theaters.

❖ The West End

The West End is known for its theaters and shopping, and is home to many of the city's most famous theaters, such as the Royal Opera House and the London Palladium.

❖ Camden

Camden is a trendy and bohemian neighborhood, known for its markets, music venues, and alternative culture.

❖ Notting Hill

Notting Hill is a fashionable and upscale neighborhood, known for its colorful houses and the Notting Hill Carnival, the largest street festival in Europe.

❖ Shoreditch

Shoreditch is a trendy and creative neighborhood, known for its street art, independent shops, and vibrant nightlife.

❖ The East End

The East End is a diverse and historic neighborhood, known for its markets, such as Columbia Road Flower Market, and its working-class roots. It is also home to a number of iconic landmarks, such as the Tower Bridge and the Tower of London.

❖ Southwark

Southwark is a diverse and vibrant neighborhood, located on the south bank of the Thames. It is home to a number of cultural institutions, such as the Tate Modern and the Globe Theatre, and is known for its street food and markets.

❖ The South Bank

The South Bank is a cultural hub, located on the south bank of the Thames. It is home to a number of theaters, galleries, and music venues, as well as the London Eye, one of the city's most iconic landmarks.

❖ Greenwich

Greenwich is a historic neighborhood, located on the south bank of the Thames. It is home to the Royal Observatory, the Prime Meridian, and the Cutty Sark, a 19th-century sailing ship.

❖ Hammersmith and Fulham

Hammersmith and Fulham is a residential neighborhood, located in west London. It is known for its shopping centers, such as Westfield London, and its green spaces, such as Fulham Palace Gardens.

Tips for Navigating the City

London is a vibrant and exciting city that offers something for everyone. Whether you are visiting for the first time or are a seasoned traveler, navigating this bustling metropolis can be a bit overwhelming. Here are some tips to help you make the most of your trip to London:

Plan ahead: London is a busy city, so it's a good idea to plan your trip in advance. Research the attractions you want to see, book your accommodation and transportation, and make any necessary reservations. This will help you make the most of your time in the city and avoid disappointment.

Use public transportation: London has an excellent public transportation system, including the Underground (also known as the "Tube"), buses, and overground trains. These are often the quickest and most convenient way to get around the city. You can purchase an Oyster card, which allows you to pay for your journeys on all forms of public transportation in London.

Stay safe: London is generally a safe city, but it's always a good idea to be aware of your surroundings and take basic safety precautions. Keep an eye on your belongings, and be mindful of pickpockets in crowded areas. Avoid walking alone at night in unfamiliar areas, and consider using licensed black cabs or ride-sharing apps instead.

Respect local customs: London is a diverse and multicultural city, so it's important to be respectful of local customs and traditions. This includes being mindful of your behavior in public spaces and following local laws and regulations.

Learn some basic phrases: While many Londoners speak English, it can be helpful to learn some basic phrases in the local language. "Thank you", "please", and "excuse me" are a few useful phrases to know.

Take advantage of discounts: London can be an expensive city, but there are many ways to save money on your trip. Consider purchasing a discount pass for attractions, such as the London Pass, or look for deals on things like meals and transportation.

Be flexible: London is a constantly evolving city, so it's important to be flexible and open to new experiences. Don't be afraid to stray from your itinerary and try something new — you never know what hidden gems you might discover.

Use the Citymapper app: This handy app is a must-have for getting around London. It provides real-time updates on public transportation, including the Tube and buses, and can even help you plan your route and estimate travel times.

Get a SIM card: If you're planning to use your phone to navigate the city, it might be worth getting a local SIM card. This will save you money on international roaming fees and ensure that you have reliable connectivity while you're in London.

Stay near a Tube station: London is a sprawling city, so it's a good idea to stay in an area that is well-connected by the Tube. This will make it easier to get around and visit the city's top attractions.

Take a walking tour: One of the best ways to get to know London is by foot. Consider joining a walking tour to explore the city and learn about its history and culture.

Go off the beaten path: While London's top attractions are certainly worth a visit, don't forget to explore the city's lesser-known neighborhoods and hidden gems. From trendy markets to historic pubs, there's always something new to discover in London.

Try the local food: London is home to a diverse range of cuisines, from traditional English fare to global flavors. Don't be afraid to try something new – you might just discover your new favorite dish.

Pack light: London is a bustling city, so it's a good idea to pack light to make it easier to get around. Consider bringing a small suitcase or backpack that you can easily carry on public transportation.

Take a river cruise: The River Thames winds through the heart of London, offering a unique perspective on the city. Consider taking a river cruise to see the city's top landmarks from a different angle.

Use contactless payment: Many London businesses accept contactless payment, which allows you to pay for purchases using your debit or credit card by simply tapping it against a reader. This is a convenient and secure way to pay in London.

Watch out for peak hours: London's public transportation can get very crowded during peak hours (generally 7:30-9:30am and 4:30-6:30pm on weekdays). If possible, try to avoid traveling during these times or consider using alternative modes of transportation.

Use the "Mind the Gap" announcement: The "Mind the Gap" announcement is a famous feature of the London Underground, warning passengers to be careful when crossing the gap between the train and the platform. Be sure to listen for this announcement when boarding and exiting trains, as it can help prevent accidents.

Try the local markets: London is home to a number of bustling markets, from the iconic Borough Market to the trendy Camden Market. These are great places to try local food, pick up souvenirs, and experience London's vibrant street culture.

Take a break from the city: London is a great city to explore, but it can be overwhelming at times. If you need a break from the hustle and bustle, consider taking a trip to one of the city's many green spaces. From the beautiful gardens at Kew to the sprawling Hampstead Heath, there are plenty of peaceful spots to relax and recharge in London.

CONCLUSION

London is a vibrant and diverse city with a rich history and culture. From its iconic landmarks and bustling streets to its world-renowned museums and theaters, there's something for everyone in the city. Whether you're interested in exploring the city's rich history, indulging in its culinary delights, or taking in a show, London has something to offer.

As you begin your journey to London, be sure to plan ahead and make the most of your time in the city. Use the tips provided above to navigate your way around the city, and be sure to explore its many neighborhoods and hidden gems. With a little planning and some local knowledge, you'll be well on your way to making the most of your trip to London.

CHAPTER 2

GETTING AROUND LONDON

London is a large and bustling city, so having a good understanding of the transportation options available can help make your trip more enjoyable. Here are some options for getting around London:

1. The Underground (also known as the "Tube")

The London Underground is a fast and efficient way to get around the city. It consists of 11 lines that cover most of London, and there are also several overground trains that connect the city. You can purchase an Oyster card, which allows you to pay for your journeys on all forms of public transportation in London, or you can pay with a contactless debit or credit card.

2. Buses

London's bus network is extensive and covers most of the city. Buses run frequently and are a good option for getting around, especially if you're visiting areas not served by the Underground. You can pay for your journey with an Oyster card or contactless payment.

3. Taxis

London is home to a fleet of licensed black cabs, which can be hailed on the street or at a designated taxi rank. You can also use ride-sharing apps like Uber to book a ride.

4. Walking

London is a walkable city, and many of the city's top attractions are within easy walking distance of each other. Walking is a great way to explore the city and see the sights. Just be sure to stay safe and aware of your surroundings, especially in busy areas.

5. Bicycle

If you're feeling fit and adventurous, you might consider exploring London by bicycle. The city has a network of dedicated bike lanes and a bike-sharing program called Santander Cycles, which allows you to rent a bike for short journeys around the city.

6. River services

If you're looking for a unique way to see the city, consider taking a river service. Thames Clippers operates a fleet of high-speed catamarans that run between central London and locations along the Thames, including the Tower of London and Greenwich.

7. Trams

London's tram network is a good option for getting around the city, especially if you're visiting areas not served by the Underground. Trams run frequently and offer a comfortable and convenient way to get around.

8. National Rail

If you're planning to visit destinations outside of London, you might consider using the National Rail network. This network of trains connects London to cities and towns across the country, making it a convenient way to explore the region.

9. Coaches

If you're planning to visit destinations further afield, you might consider taking a coach. National Express operates a network of coaches that connect London to cities and towns across the UK. Coaches are a budget-friendly option for long-distance travel.

10. Rental cars

If you prefer to have your own transportation, you might consider renting a car. Keep in mind that driving in London can be challenging due to the city's busy streets and complex road system, so it's a good idea to familiarize yourself with the rules of the road before you set off.

Tips for Using Public Transport in London

Using public transportation is a convenient and efficient way to get around London, but it can be intimidating if you're not familiar with the system. Here are some tips to help you make the most of your public transportation experience in London:

Purchase an Oyster card: An Oyster card is a smart card that allows you to pay for your journeys on all forms of public transportation in London, including the Underground (also known as the "Tube"), buses, and overground trains. You can purchase an Oyster card at any Underground station, or online in advance of your trip.

Know your fare zones: London is divided into fare zones, and the cost of your journey depends on which zones you travel through. Be sure to check the fare zones before you travel to ensure that you have the correct fare.

Plan your route in advance: It's a good idea to plan your route in advance to ensure that you know which lines and stations you need to use. You can use the Transport for London website or the Citymapper app to plan your journey and estimate travel times.

Stand on the right: When using the escalators on the Underground, be sure to stand on the right side to allow room for those in a hurry to pass on the left. This is a common practice in London and will help keep the flow of traffic moving smoothly.

Look for "Mind the Gap" announcements: The "Mind the Gap" announcement is a famous feature of the London Underground, warning passengers to be careful when crossing the gap between the train and the platform. Be sure to listen for this announcement when boarding and exiting trains, as it can help prevent accidents.

Use contactless payment: Many London businesses accept contactless payment, which allows you to pay for purchases using your debit or credit card by simply tapping it against a reader. This is a convenient and secure way to pay for your journeys on public transportation in London.

Know the rules: It's important to familiarize yourself with the rules of the London Underground and other forms of public transportation. This includes standing to the right on escalators, not eating or drinking on the trains, and not blocking the doors when boarding or exiting.

Be aware of peak hours: London's public transportation can get very crowded during peak hours (generally 7:30-9:30am and 4:30-6:30pm on weekdays). If possible, try to avoid traveling during these times or consider using alternative modes of transportation.

Keep an eye on your belongings: Like any busy city, London can be a target for pickpockets, so it's important to keep an eye on your belongings while using public transportation. Be sure to keep your valuables close to you, and consider using a bag with a secure closure to keep your belongings safe.

Use the "Help Point" intercoms: If you need help or have any questions while using London's public transportation, look for the "Help Point" intercoms located at most Underground and overground stations. These intercoms allow you to speak to a member of staff who can assist you with your query.

Consider purchasing a Travelcard: If you're planning to use public transportation extensively during your trip to London, you might consider purchasing a Travelcard. This allows you unlimited travel within specific fare zones for a fixed period of time, making it a convenient and cost-effective option for those who plan to use public transportation frequently.

Know your exits: When using the Underground, it's a good idea to familiarize yourself with the layout of the station and the location of the exits. This will make it easier to find your way once you reach your destination.

Use the "Step Free" routes: If you have mobility issues or are traveling with young children, you might consider using the "Step Free" routes available on the Underground and overground. These routes are designed to be more accessible and have fewer steps, making it easier to get around the city.

Take advantage of discounts: If you're planning to use public transportation extensively during your trip, you might consider purchasing a discount pass. Options include the London Pass, which offers unlimited travel on the Underground and overground, as well as discounts on attractions, and the Oyster Visitor Card, which offers discounted fares for tourists.

Stay safe: As with any busy city, it's important to be aware of your surroundings and take basic safety precautions when using public transportation in London. Be mindful of your belongings, and consider using licensed black cabs or ride-sharing apps instead of walking alone at night in unfamiliar areas.

Information on Sightseeing Passes and Discounts
If you're planning to do a lot of sightseeing during your trip to London, you might consider purchasing a sightseeing pass or discount card to save money and make the most of your time in the city. Here are some options to consider:

1. The London Pass

The London Pass is a sightseeing pass that offers unlimited travel on the Underground and overground, as well as discounts on over 80 top attractions in London. This includes popular sights like the Tower of London, Buckingham Palace, and the London Eye. The

London Pass also includes a guidebook and the option to skip the line at certain attractions.

2. The Oyster Visitor Card

The Oyster Visitor Card is a smart card that offers discounted fares on the Underground, overground, buses, and trams in London. This is a good option for those who plan to use public transportation extensively during their trip. The Oyster Visitor Card also offers discounts on attractions and restaurants.

3. The Go London Card

The Go London Card is a discount card that offers discounts on over 60 top attractions in London, as well as discounts on restaurants, shops, and entertainment. The Go London Card also includes a guidebook and the option to skip the line at certain attractions.

4. The London City Pass

The London City Pass is a discount card that offers discounts on over 50 top attractions in London, as well as discounts on restaurants, shops, and entertainment. The London City Pass also includes a guidebook and the option to skip the line at certain attractions.

5. The London Explorer Pass

The London Explorer Pass is a flexible sightseeing pass that allows you to choose the attractions you want to visit and pay one discounted price. This is a good option for those who want to customize their sightseeing itinerary.

6 Tips to Consider When Choosing a Sightseeing Pass or Discount Card for your Trip to London
1. Consider your travel style

Different sightseeing passes and discount cards are better suited to different travel styles. If you prefer to plan your own itinerary and have flexibility, a discount card like the Go London Card or the London City Pass might be a good option. If you prefer to have everything planned out in advance, a pass like the London Pass or the London Explorer Pass might be a better fit.

2. Compare prices

Before you purchase a sightseeing pass or discount card, be sure to compare prices and do the math to see which option offers the best value for your trip. Consider the cost of individual tickets and the discounts offered by each pass or card to determine the best option for your budget.

3. Check the expiration date

Some sightseeing passes and discount cards have expiration dates, so be sure to check the fine print before purchasing. This will help ensure that you have enough time to use the pass or card during your trip.

4. Know what's included

Different sightseeing passes and discount cards offer different levels of discounts and perks, so be sure to read the fine print and understand what's included before making a decision. Some passes and cards offer discounts on a wide range of attractions, while others are more limited in scope. It's a good idea to make a list of the attractions you want to visit and compare them to the discounts offered by each pass or card to determine the best option for your trip.

5. Check for exclusions

Some sightseeing passes and discount cards have exclusions or blackout dates, so be sure to check the fine print before making a decision. This will help ensure that you can use the pass or card on the dates you want to visit the attractions.

6. Consider the convenience factor

A sightseeing pass or discount card can be a convenient way to save money and plan your trip, but it's important to consider the convenience factor as well. Some passes and cards require you to redeem vouchers or tickets at each attraction, while others offer more seamless access. Consider which option is best for your travel style and needs.

CONCLUSION

No matter which transportation option you choose, it's important to plan ahead and allow plenty of time to get to your destination. The city can be busy, so it's a good idea to factor in additional time for unexpected delays. With these options in mind, you'll be well on your way to getting around London with ease.

CHAPTER 3

ACCOMMODATION IN LONDON

London is a popular tourist destination, so it's important to plan your accommodation in advance to ensure that you have a comfortable and convenient place to stay during your trip.

Tips for Finding and Booking Accommodation in London
Here are some tips for finding accommodation in London:

1. Decide on a location

London is a large and diverse city, so it's a good idea to consider the location of your accommodation before booking. Popular neighborhoods include central London, which is home to many of the city's top attractions, and the trendy neighborhoods of Shoreditch, Notting Hill, and Soho.

2. Choose your type of accommodation

London offers a range of accommodation options to suit different budgets and preferences. These include hotels, guest houses, hostels, and vacation rentals. Be sure to consider the amenities and services offered by each option to determine the best fit for your needs.

3. Book in advance

London is a popular tourist destination, so it's a good idea to book your accommodation in advance to ensure that you have a place to stay. This is especially important during peak tourist seasons, when availability can be limited.

4. Consider the price

Accommodation in London can vary in price, so it's a good idea to consider your budget when making a booking. Be sure to compare prices and read reviews to find the best value for your money.

5. Check the cancellation policy

Before making a booking, be sure to read the cancellation policy to understand your options if you need to change or cancel your reservation. Some accommodations offer flexible cancellation policies, while others may charge a fee for changes or cancellations.

6. Look for deals and discounts

There are often deals and discounts available on accommodation in London, so it's a good idea to keep an eye out for these when booking. Some options to consider include booking during the off-season, signing up for loyalty programs, and looking for last-minute deals.

7. Consider using a booking site

Booking sites like Expedia, Hotels.com, and Booking.com offer a wide range of accommodation options in London and can be a convenient way to compare prices and amenities. Be sure to read reviews and check the cancellation policy before making a booking.

8. Use Airbnb

Airbnb is a popular option for accommodation in London, and offers a range of options from private rooms to entire apartments. Be sure to read the reviews and check the cancellation policy before booking.

9. Consider a vacation rental

If you're planning a longer stay in London or are traveling with a group, you might consider a vacation rental. Options include apartments, houses, and even entire cottages, and can offer a more home-like experience.

10. Consider location

When choosing your accommodation in London, be sure to consider the location and proximity to the attractions you want to visit. This can help save time and money on transportation.

11. Consider the amenities

When choosing your accommodation in London, be sure to consider the amenities that are important to you. Options to consider include a gym, pool, or on-site restaurant.

12. Check the reviews

Before making a booking, be sure to read the reviews left by previous guests to get an idea of the quality of the accommodation and the level of service provided.

13. Consider the location of the accommodation in relation to public transportation

London has an extensive public transportation system, so it's a good idea to consider the location of your accommodation in relation to the nearest subway, bus, or train station. This can make it easier to get around the city.

14. Consider the size of the accommodation

If you're traveling with a group or plan to stay in London for an extended period of time, you might consider a larger accommodation option like a vacation rental or apartment. This can provide more space and privacy than a traditional hotel room.

15. Consider the length of your stay

If you're planning a longer stay in London, you might consider a serviced apartment or vacation rental, which can offer more space and amenities than a traditional hotel room.

Recommendations for Different Budget Ranges when in London

Here are some recommendations for different budget ranges:

1. Budget

If you're looking for a budget-friendly option, you might consider a hostel or a budget hotel. Hostels offer dormitory-style rooms and shared facilities and can be a great option for solo travelers or those on a tight budget.

Some popular hostels in London include YHA Oxford Street, Generator Hostel London, and The YHA. Budget hotels offer private rooms with en-suite bathrooms at a lower price point than luxury hotels. Some popular budget hotels in London include Premier Inn, Travelodge, and ibis budget.

2. Mid-Range

If you're looking for something a little more luxurious, but still affordable, there are plenty of mid-range options in London. These might include boutique hotels, bed and breakfasts, or vacation rentals.

Boutique hotels offer a more personalized experience and often have a unique design aesthetic. Some popular mid-range hotels in London include The Z Hotel Oxford Street, The Z Hotel Tottenham Court Road, and The Good Morning Hostel. Vacation rentals can offer a more home-like experience and come in a range of sizes to suit different group sizes. Some popular vacation rental sites for London include Airbnb, HomeAway, and VRBO.

3. Luxury

If you're looking to splurge on your trip to London, there are plenty of luxurious accommodation options to choose from.

Luxury hotels in London offer top-notch amenities and services, including luxurious accommodations, spa and fitness facilities, and a range of dining options. Some popular luxury hotels in London include The Ritz, The Dorchester, The Mandarin Oriental, and The Four Seasons.

30 Best Expensive Hotels to Stay During your Trip to London
The Ritz London: This iconic luxury hotel is located in the heart of London and offers luxurious accommodations, a spa and fitness center, and a range of dining options.

The Dorchester: Located in the prestigious Mayfair neighborhood, The Dorchester offers luxurious accommodations, a spa and fitness center, and a range of dining options.

The Mandarin Oriental: This luxury hotel is located in the heart of London and offers luxurious accommodations, a spa and fitness center, and a range of dining options.

The Four Seasons Hotel London at Park Lane: Located in the heart of London, this luxury hotel offers luxurious accommodations, a spa and fitness center, and a range of dining options.

The Lanesborough: This luxury hotel is located in the heart of London and offers luxurious accommodations, a spa and fitness center, and a range of dining options.

The Savoy: Located in the heart of London, this luxury hotel offers luxurious accommodations, a spa and fitness center, and a range of dining options.

The Shard: This luxury hotel is located in the iconic Shard building and offers luxurious accommodations, a spa and fitness center, and a range of dining options.

The Rosewood London: Located in the heart of London, this luxury hotel offers luxurious accommodations, a spa and fitness center, and a range of dining options.

The Plaza on the River Club and Residence: This luxury hotel is located on the Thames riverfront and offers luxurious accommodations, a spa and fitness center, and a range of dining options.

The St. Pancras Renaissance London Hotel: Located in the iconic St. Pancras train station, this luxury hotel offers luxurious accommodations, a spa and fitness center, and a range of dining options.

The Grosvenor House, A JW Marriott Hotel: Located in the heart of London, this luxury hotel offers luxurious accommodations, a spa and fitness center, and a range of dining options.

The Park Tower Knightsbridge, A Luxury Collection Hotel: Located in the fashionable Knightsbridge neighborhood, this luxury hotel offers luxurious accommodations, a spa and fitness center, and a range of dining options.

The Langham, London: This iconic luxury hotel is located in the heart of London and offers luxurious accommodations, a spa and fitness center, and a range of dining options.

The InterContinental London - The O2: Located in the Greenwich Peninsula, this luxury hotel offers luxurious accommodations, a spa and fitness center, and a range of dining options.

The Royal Horseguards: This luxury hotel is located in the heart of London and offers luxurious accommodations, a spa and fitness center, and a range of dining options.

The Claridge's: Located in the fashionable Mayfair neighborhood, this luxury hotel offers luxurious accommodations, a spa and fitness center, and a range of dining options.

The May Fair Hotel: Located in the heart of London, this luxury hotel offers luxurious accommodations, a spa and fitness center, and a range of dining options..

The London EDITION: Located in the fashionable Fitzrovia neighborhood, this luxury hotel offers luxurious accommodations, a spa and fitness center, and a range of dining options.

The Corinthia Hotel London: Located in the heart of London, this luxury hotel offers luxurious accommodations, a spa and fitness center, and a range of dining options.

NOTE: Keep in mind that the cost, reviews, amenities, and addresses of these hotels may change over time, and it's a good idea to check with the hotels directly or use a booking site to confirm current prices and availability.

14 Best Affordable Hotels to Stay During your Trip to London

YHA Oxford Street: This budget-friendly hostel is located in the heart of London and offers private rooms and dormitory-style accommodations. Amenities include a shared kitchen, a common area, and a 24-hour front desk.

Premier Inn London City (Aldgate): This budget hotel is located in the trendy Aldgate neighborhood and offers private rooms with en-suite bathrooms. Amenities include a restaurant, a bar, and a 24-hour front desk.

Travelodge London Central City Road: This budget hotel is located in the trendy Shoreditch neighborhood and offers private rooms with en-suite bathrooms. Amenities include a 24-hour front desk and a vending machine.

Generator Hostel London: This budget-friendly hostel is located in the trendy King's Cross neighborhood and offers private rooms and dormitory-style accommodations. Amenities include a shared kitchen, a common area, and a 24-hour front desk.

Ibis budget London City: This budget hotel is located in the trendy Shoreditch neighborhood and offers private rooms with en-suite bathrooms. Amenities include a 24-hour front desk and a vending machine.

Premier Inn London City (Aldgate East): This budget hotel is located in the trendy Aldgate East neighborhood and offers private rooms with en-suite bathrooms. Amenities include a restaurant, a bar, and a 24-hour front desk.

Premier Inn London City (Barbican): This budget hotel is located in the trendy Barbican neighborhood and offers private rooms with en-suite bathrooms. Amenities include a restaurant, a bar, and a 24-hour front desk.

Premier Inn London City (Liverpool Street): This budget hotel is located in the trendy Liverpool Street neighborhood and offers private rooms with en-suite bathrooms. Amenities include a restaurant, a bar, and a 24-hour front desk.

Premier Inn London City (Old Street): This budget hotel is located in the trendy Old Street neighborhood and offers private rooms with en-suite bathrooms. Amenities include a restaurant, a bar, and a 24-hour front desk.

Premier Inn London City (Shoreditch): This budget hotel is located in the trendy Shoreditch neighborhood and offers private rooms with en-suite bathrooms. Amenities include a restaurant, a bar, and a 24-hour front desk.

Premier Inn London City (Tower Hill): This budget hotel is located in the trendy Tower Hill neighborhood and offers private rooms with en-suite bathrooms. Amenities include a restaurant, a bar, and a 24-hour front desk.

Premier Inn London City (Aldgate): This budget hotel is located in the trendy Aldgate neighborhood and offers private rooms with en-suite bathrooms. Amenities include a restaurant, a bar, and a 24-hour front desk.

Premier Inn London City (Cannon Street): This budget hotel is located in the trendy Cannon Street neighborhood and offers private rooms with en-suite bathrooms. Amenities include a restaurant, a bar, and a 24-hour front desk.

Premier Inn London City (Moorgate): This budget hotel is located in the trendy Moorgate neighborhood and offers private rooms with en-suite bathrooms. Amenities include a restaurant, a bar, and a 24-hour front desk.

Other Accommodation Options you Should Look into When in London

1. Hostels

Hostels are a budget-friendly accommodation option that offer dormitory-style rooms and shared facilities. They can be a great option for solo travelers or those on a tight budget. Some popular hostels in London include YHA Oxford Street, Generator Hostel London, and The YHA.

2. Vacation Rentals

If you're planning a longer stay in London or are traveling with a group, you might consider a vacation rental. Options include apartments, houses, and even entire cottages, and can offer a more home-like experience. Some popular vacation rental sites for London include Airbnb, HomeAway, and VRBO.

3. Bed and Breakfasts

Bed and breakfasts are a popular accommodation option in London, offering a more personal and homely experience. They typically offer private rooms with shared facilities and a hearty breakfast each morning. Some popular bed and breakfasts in London include The Good Morning Hostel, The Z Hotel Oxford Street, and The Z Hotel Tottenham Court Road.

When choosing a hostel or vacation rental, be sure to consider the location, amenities, and price. It's also a good idea to read reviews left by previous guests to get an idea of the quality of the accommodation and the level of service provided.

CONCLUSION

Finding accommodation in London can be a challenging task due to the high demand and limited availability of housing. However, with some research and planning, it is possible to find a suitable place to stay that meets your needs and budget. Some options to consider include renting a flat or house, staying in a hostel or hotel, or finding a room in a shared house or apartment.

It is also important to consider the location of your accommodation and whether it is convenient for your daily activities and commute. By weighing the pros and cons of each option and taking the time to research and compare prices, you can find the best accommodation solution for your stay in London.

CHAPTER 4

EATING AND DRINKING IN LONDON

Overview of London's Food Scene

London is a diverse and vibrant city with a rich food culture that reflects the city's multicultural and cosmopolitan nature. From traditional British pub grub to international cuisine from every corner of the globe, London's food scene is truly diverse and exciting.

One of the standout features of London's food scene is the abundance of markets and street food stalls offering a wide range of cuisines and flavors. Borough Market, for example, is a popular destination for foodies and tourists alike, offering an impressive selection of fresh produce, artisanal cheeses, and international street food. Other markets worth checking out include the Old Spitalfields Market, the Camden Market, and the Brick Lane Market.

In addition to markets, London is also home to a vast array of restaurants, cafes, and pubs serving up a diverse range of cuisines. From Michelin-starred fine dining restaurants to casual bistros and cafes, there is something to suit every taste and budget. Some popular neighborhoods for dining out include Soho, Mayfair, and Notting Hill, which are known for their diverse and vibrant food scenes.

Another highlight of London's food scene is the city's thriving street food movement. From gourmet burgers and artisanal pizzas to authentic curries and falafel wraps, London's street food scene has something to offer every food lover. Some popular street food destinations include the Street Food Union at Old Spitalfields Market and the Street Feast market in Dalston.

London's food scene is a diverse and exciting melting pot of flavors and cuisines that reflects the city's multicultural and cosmopolitan nature. Whether you're in the mood for a traditional British pub meal, international cuisine, or a gourmet street food experience, London has something to offer every food lover.

Best Restaurants to Visit in London
The Fat Duck - This three-Michelin-starred restaurant in Bray, Berkshire, is run by celebrated chef Heston Blumenthal. The Fat Duck is known for its innovative and experimental dishes, such as the famous "Sound of the Sea," a seafood dish served with an iPod playing the sound of waves crashing on the shore.

Dinner by Heston Blumenthal - This two-Michelin-starred restaurant in Knightsbridge is also run by chef Heston Blumenthal, and is known for its historical dishes inspired by medieval and Renaissance cooking.

The Ledbury - This two-Michelin-starred restaurant in Notting Hill is run by chef Brett Graham, and is known for its modern European cuisine and exceptional wine list.

The Clove Club - This one-Michelin-starred restaurant in Shoreditch is known for its innovative and modern British cuisine, as well as its exceptional wine list.

The River Café - This iconic Italian restaurant in Hammersmith is known for its fresh, seasonal ingredients and classic Italian dishes.

The Square - This two-Michelin-starred restaurant in Mayfair is known for its modern French cuisine and exceptional wine list.

The Ritz London - This luxury hotel in Mayfair is home to the two-Michelin-starred Ritz Restaurant, known for its classic French cuisine and opulent dining room.

The Goring - This luxury hotel in Belgravia is home to the one-Michelin-starred Dining Room, known for its modern British cuisine and elegant setting.

The Ivy - This iconic London restaurant in Covent Garden is known for its classic British cuisine and celebrity clientele.

The Wolseley - This grand cafe in Mayfair is known for its classic European cuisine and elegant setting.

The Chiltern Firehouse - This trendy restaurant in Marylebone is known for its modern American cuisine and celebrity clientele.

The Dorchester - This luxury hotel in Mayfair is home to the three-Michelin-starred Alain Ducasse at The Dorchester, known for its modern French cuisine and opulent setting.

The Mandarin Oriental - This luxury hotel in Knightsbridge is home to the two-Michelin-starred Dinner by Heston Blumenthal, known for its historical dishes inspired by medieval and Renaissance cooking.

The Savoy - This luxury hotel in Covent Garden is home to the two-Michelin-starred Gordon Ramsay at The Savoy, known for its modern French cuisine and elegant setting.

The Berkeley - This luxury hotel in Knightsbridge is home to the one-Michelin-starred Marcus, known for its modern European cuisine and exceptional wine list.

The RAC Club - This private members club in Pall Mall is home to the one-Michelin-starred Luca, known for its modern Italian cuisine and elegant setting.

SushiSamba - This trendy restaurant in the City is known for its fusion of Japanese, Brazilian, and Peruvian cuisines.

Nobu - This trendy restaurant in Mayfair is known for its fusion of Japanese and Peruvian cuisines.

Benares - This one-Michelin-starred restaurant in Mayfair is known for its modern Indian cuisine and exceptional wine list.

The Cinnamon Club - This one-Michelin-starred restaurant in Westminster is known for its modern Indian cuisine and elegant setting.

The Lanesborough - This luxury hotel in Knightsbridge is home to the one-Michelin-starred Céleste, known for its modern French cuisine and opulent setting.

Quaglino's - This iconic restaurant in Mayfair is known for its modern European cuisine and lively atmosphere.

The Jugged Hare - This popular pub in the City is known for its excellent selection of craft beers and traditional British pub grub.

The Gilbert Scott - This trendy restaurant in King's Cross is known for its modern British cuisine and beautiful setting inside the historic St Pancras Hotel.

The Wolseley - This grand cafe in Mayfair is known for its classic European cuisine and elegant setting.

The Ivy Chelsea Garden - This trendy restaurant in Chelsea is known for its modern British cuisine and beautiful outdoor garden.

The Delaunay - This popular cafe in Covent Garden is known for its classic European cuisine and elegant setting.

The Ledbury - This two-Michelin-starred restaurant in Notting Hill is known for its modern European cuisine and exceptional wine list.

The Ritz London - This luxury hotel in Mayfair is home to the two-Michelin-starred Ritz Restaurant, known for its classic French cuisine and opulent dining room.

Delicious Meals to try out in London

Fish and Chips - No trip to London would be complete without trying this classic British dish. Consisting of battered and fried fish served with chips (fries), fish and chips is a staple of British cuisine and can be found at pubs and takeaways all over the city.

Roast Dinner - Another classic British dish, a roast dinner typically consists of roast meat (such as beef, lamb, or chicken), roast potatoes, vegetables, and gravy. It is often served on Sundays and can be found at pubs and restaurants all over London.

Pie and Mash - This traditional London dish consists of a savory pie (usually made with meat and vegetables) served with mashed potatoes and a green parsley sauce known as "liquor." It can be found at pie and mash shops all over the city.

Curry - London has a thriving Indian food scene, and curry is a popular choice for both locals and tourists. From classic dishes like chicken tikka masala and lamb vindaloo to more regional specialties like Goan fish curry and Tamil Nadu chicken curry, there is a curry to suit every taste.

Dim Sum - London has a large Chinese population, and as a result, there are many excellent Chinese restaurants serving up delicious dim sum. Dim sum consists of small steamed or fried dumplings filled with meat, seafood, or vegetables, and is traditionally served for breakfast or lunch.

Afternoon Tea - This quintessentially British experience involves indulging in a selection of sandwiches, pastries, and scones, accompanied by a pot of tea. Afternoon tea can be found at hotels, restaurants, and tea shops all over London.

Gastropub Grub - London is home to many excellent gastropubs, which are pubs that serve high-quality, restaurant-standard food. From artisanal pizzas and gourmet burgers to modern takes on classic British dishes, gastropub grub is a great way to experience the best of British cuisine.

Street Food - London's street food scene is thriving, with markets and street food stalls offering a wide range of cuisines and flavors. From gourmet burgers and artisanal pizzas to authentic curries and falafel wraps, there is something to suit every taste.

Afternoon Tea - This quintessentially British experience involves indulging in a selection of sandwiches, pastries, and scones, accompanied by a pot of tea. Afternoon tea can be found at hotels, restaurants, and tea shops all over London.

Peking Duck - This classic Chinese dish involves roasting a duck until the skin is crisp and the meat is tender, and then serving it with thin pancakes, scallions, and hoisin sauce. Peking duck can be found at many Chinese restaurants in London.

Full English Breakfast - This hearty breakfast dish consists of bacon, eggs, sausage, baked beans, grilled tomato, and black pudding, and is a staple of British cuisine. It can be found at cafes and pubs all over London.

Roast Beef and Yorkshire Pudding - This classic British dish consists of roast beef served with roast potatoes, vegetables, and a large Yorkshire pudding (a savory pastry made with egg and flour). It is a popular choice for Sunday lunch and can be found at pubs and restaurants all over the city.

Ploughman's Lunch - This traditional British pub meal consists of a selection of cheese, pickles, and crusty bread, and is often served with a pint of ale. It is a great option for a casual lunch or dinner and can be found at pubs all over London.

Sushi - London has a thriving Japanese food scene, and sushi is a popular choice for both locals and tourists. From classic rolls like California rolls and spicy tuna rolls to more unusual options like squid ink sushi and uni (sea urchin), there is a sushi dish to suit every taste.

Nando's - This popular chain of Portuguese-style chicken restaurants can be found all over London, and is known for its spicy peri-peri sauce and flame-grilled chicken.

Falafel Wrap - London has a thriving street food scene, and falafel wraps are a popular choice for a quick and tasty meal on the go. These wraps are made with falafel balls (deep-fried balls of ground chickpeas and spices), lettuce, tomato, and a variety of sauces, and can be found at street food stalls all over the city.

Afternoon Tea - This quintessentially British experience involves indulging in a selection of sandwiches, pastries, and scones, accompanied by a pot of tea. Afternoon tea can be found at hotels, restaurants, and tea shops all over London.

Noodle Soup - London has a thriving Chinese food scene, and noodle soup is a popular choice for a quick and satisfying meal. From classic dishes like wonton noodle soup and beef noodle soup to more unusual options like spicy Szechuan-style noodles and curry-flavored noodles, there is a noodle soup to suit every taste.

Pint of Ale - London is home to many excellent pubs, and a pint of ale is a classic choice for a casual drink. From classic English ales to more modern craft beers, there is an ale to suit every taste.

Sunday Roast - This traditional British dish typically consists of roast meat (such as beef, lamb, or chicken), roast potatoes, vegetables, and gravy, and is often served on Sundays. It can be found at pubs and restaurants all over London.

Bubble and Squeak - This classic British dish is made with leftover vegetables (such as mashed potatoes and cabbage) that are fried together until crispy. It is often served with roast meat and gravy and is a popular choice for a hearty breakfast or brunch.

Full English Breakfast - This hearty breakfast dish consists of bacon, eggs, sausage, baked beans, grilled tomato, and black pudding, and is a staple of British cuisine. It can be found at cafes and pubs all over London.

Beef Wellington - This classic British dish consists of a fillet of beef wrapped in pastry and baked until tender. It is often served with roast potatoes, vegetables, and gravy and can be found at pubs and restaurants all over the city.

Cottage Pie - This classic British dish consists of minced meat (usually beef) and vegetables topped with mashed potatoes and baked until golden and bubbly. It is a popular choice for a hearty and comforting meal and can be found at pubs and restaurants all over London.

Bangers and Mash - This classic British dish consists of sausage (referred to as "bangers") served with mashed potatoes and gravy. It is a simple and hearty meal that can be found at pubs and restaurants all over the city.

Black Pudding - This traditional British sausage is made with pork blood and oats and is often served as part of a full English breakfast or as a standalone dish. It can be found at pubs and restaurants all over London.

Cornish Pasty - This traditional British savory pastry is made with minced meat and vegetables and is a popular choice for a quick and satisfying meal. It can be found at bakeries and pubs all over London.

Scotch Egg - This classic British snack consists of a hard-boiled egg wrapped in sausage meat and breadcrumbs and deep-fried until golden. It is a popular choice for a quick and satisfying snack and can be found at pubs and convenience stores all over the city.

Sausage Roll - This classic British snack consists of sausage meat wrapped in puff pastry and baked until golden and flaky. It is a popular choice for a quick and satisfying snack and can be found at bakeries and convenience stores all over London.

Tips for Finding Good Value Meals during your Stay in London
London is a vibrant and exciting city, with a wide variety of dining options to choose from. However, as with any major city, prices can sometimes be steep, especially when it comes to meals. If you're looking for good value meals during your stay in London, here are some tips to help you out:

Look for deals and discounts: Many restaurants in London offer special deals and discounts on certain days of the week or at certain times of day. For example, some restaurants offer "early bird" specials for diners who come in before a certain time, or "happy hour" discounts on drinks. Keep an eye out for these deals, as they can help you save money on your meals.

Consider eating at local markets: London is home to a number of vibrant local markets, such as Borough Market and Camden Market, where you can find a wide variety of food options at affordable prices. These markets often feature street food stalls offering dishes from around the world, as well as local specialties.

Check out ethnic neighborhoods: London is a diverse city, and you'll find a variety of ethnic neighborhoods throughout the city, each with its own unique culinary offerings. For example, the Chinatown neighborhood in Soho is known for its affordable and delicious Chinese food, while the Curry Hill neighborhood in East London is home to a number of great Indian restaurants.

Look for "set menus": Many restaurants in London offer set menus, which typically include a starter, main course, and dessert for a fixed price. These set menus can be a good value, especially if you're looking for a more formal dining experience.

Consider eating at pubs: Pubs are a staple of British culture, and many of them offer good value meals at affordable prices. You'll often find pub food such as burgers, fish and chips, and roast dinners on the menu, as well as a wide selection of beers and other drinks.

Don't be afraid to ask for a discount: If you're a student, senior citizen, or part of a large group, don't be afraid to ask the restaurant if they offer any discounts. Many restaurants are willing to offer discounts to these groups, so it never hurts to ask.

Eat at local cafes and sandwich shops: Local cafes and sandwich shops can often offer affordable meals that are still tasty and satisfying. You'll find a wide variety of options, including sandwiches, salads, soups, and pastries, at prices that are often lower than those at more formal restaurants.

Try street food: Street food is a popular and affordable option in London, with a wide variety of options to choose from. You'll find street food stalls offering everything from classic fish and chips to international cuisines like falafel, kebabs, and curries.

Eat at lunchtime: Many restaurants offer lower prices on their lunchtime menus, which can be a good option if you're looking for a more formal meal at a lower price. Keep in mind that these menus may be limited, but you'll often find a good selection of dishes at a lower price than what you'd pay at dinner.

Consider cooking for yourself: If you're staying in a vacation rental or hotel with a kitchen, consider cooking for yourself to save money on meals. You can buy groceries at local markets or supermarkets and prepare your own meals, which can be a more affordable option than eating out for every meal.

Check out food festivals: London is home to a number of food festivals throughout the year, which can be a great way to try a variety of dishes at affordable prices. These festivals often feature food stalls offering a wide range of cuisines, as well as cooking demonstrations, tastings, and other food-related events.

CONCLUSION

In conclusion, London is a city with a wide variety of dining and drinking options to choose from, with something to suit every taste and budget. From street food stalls and local markets to pubs and fine dining restaurants, there's something for everyone.

To find good value meals during your stay in London, consider looking for deals and discounts, eating at local markets and ethnic neighborhoods, and checking out set menus and pub food. You can also try eating at local cafes and sandwich shops, eating at lunchtime, cooking for yourself, or attending food festivals. With these tips, you'll be able to enjoy all that London has to offer without breaking the bank.

CHAPTER 5

SIGHTSEEING IN LONDON

London is a city rich in history, culture, and landmarks, making it the perfect destination for sightseeing. Whether you're a first-time visitor or a seasoned traveler, there's always something new to discover in London.

20 Top Attractions and Landmarks in London you wouldn't want to Miss

Here are 20 top attractions and landmarks in London that you won't want to miss:

1. Buckingham Palace

The official residence of the British monarchy, Buckingham Palace is a must-see for any visitor to London. Be sure to catch the Changing of the Guard ceremony, which takes place daily at 11:30 am.

2. Tower Bridge

This iconic bridge over the Thames is one of London's most recognizable landmarks. You can visit the Tower Bridge Exhibition to learn more about the bridge's history and get a great view from the walkways above.

3. The London Eye

This giant Ferris wheel on the South Bank of the Thames offers panoramic views of the city. It's a popular attraction, so be sure to buy tickets in advance to avoid long lines.

4. Big Ben and the Houses of Parliament

Big Ben, the iconic clock tower at the Houses of Parliament, is a must-see for any visitor to London. You can take a tour of the Houses of Parliament to learn more about the history and workings of the British government.

5. The Tower of London

This historic castle and fortress is one of London's most popular tourist attractions. You can take a tour led by a Yeoman Warder (also known as a "Beefeater") to learn about the castle's history and see the Crown Jewels.

6. St. Paul's Cathedral

This iconic cathedral is a masterpiece of Baroque architecture and a must-see for any visitor to London. You can take a tour of the cathedral to learn more about its history and architecture, or climb to the top of the dome for a breathtaking view of the city.

7. The Tate Modern

This contemporary art museum is housed in a former power station and features works by artists such as Picasso, Warhol, and Hockney.

8. The British Museum

This world-famous museum is home to a vast collection of art and artifacts from around the world, including the Rosetta Stone and the Elgin Marbles.

9. The Natural History Museum

This museum is home to a vast collection of natural history specimens, including dinosaurs, minerals, and taxidermied animals.

10. The Science Museum

This museum is a great destination for science lovers, with interactive exhibits on everything from space travel to the human body.

11. The Victoria and Albert Museum

This museum is dedicated to art and design, with a collection that spans thousands of years and includes everything from ancient artifacts to modern fashion.

12. The Thames River

A walk along the Thames is a must-do for any visitor to London. You'll see iconic landmarks such as the Tower Bridge and the Houses of Parliament, and you can also take a boat tour for a different perspective on the city.

13. The London Dungeon

This popular attraction is a interactive experience that brings London's dark history to life through actors, special effects, and live shows.

14. The London Bridge Experience

This attraction combines history and horror, with exhibits on the history of the London Bridge and live scare shows.

15. The Churchill War Rooms

This underground museum is dedicated to the life and work of Winston Churchill, and includes the Cabinet War Rooms where he directed Britain's war efforts during World War II.

16. Kensington Palace

This palace is the former home of Princess Diana and is now the residence of the Duke and Duchess of Cambridge. You can take a tour of the palace to learn more about its history and see the royal apartments.

17. The Monument

This column in the City of London was built to commemorate the Great Fire of London and offers great views of the city from the top.

18. The London Zoo

This popular attraction is home to a wide variety of animals, including lions, gorillas, and penguins.

19. The Royal Observatory

This observatory in Greenwich is home to the Prime Meridian, the line of longitude that marks the division between the Eastern and Western hemispheres. You can visit the observatory to learn about the history of timekeeping and see the world's largest refracting telescope.

20. The Royal Opera House

This iconic venue is home to the Royal Opera and the Royal Ballet, and offers a variety of performances throughout the year.

How to Plan a Sightseeing Itinerary

Planning a sightseeing itinerary in London can be a daunting task, with so many amazing attractions and landmarks to choose from. However, with a little planning and organization, you can make the most of your trip and see as much as possible. Here are some tips for planning a sightseeing itinerary in London:

Determine your interests: The first step in planning your itinerary is to think about what you're interested in seeing and doing in

London. Are you interested in history, art, culture, or science? Do you want to see iconic landmarks or explore off-the-beaten-path neighborhoods? Knowing your interests will help you narrow down your options and create an itinerary that's tailored to your needs.

Research the top attractions: Once you know what you're interested in, start researching the top attractions in London. Make a list of the landmarks and museums you want to visit, and look up information on their hours of operation, ticket prices, and any special events or exhibits that may be taking place.

Consider purchasing a tourist pass: London has a number of tourist passes that offer discounted admission to a variety of attractions. These passes can be a good value if you're planning on visiting several attractions, as they can save you money on admission fees.

Plan your route: Once you know which attractions you want to visit, start mapping out your route. Consider the location of each attraction and try to group them together to minimize travel time. You can use a map or a trip planning app to help you plan your route.

Allow for flexibility: While it's important to have a plan, it's also important to allow for some flexibility. Things may not always go as planned, and you may want to change your itinerary on the fly. Leave some room in your schedule for unplanned activities or for days when you just want to wander and explore.

Consider taking a guided tour: If you're short on time or want to make the most of your trip, consider taking a guided tour. Guided tours can be a great way to see a lot of attractions in a short amount of time, and they often include transportation and other perks.

Book tickets in advance: Many of London's top attractions, such as the Tower of London and the London Eye, can get very busy, especially during peak tourist season. To avoid long lines and ensure that you get a spot, consider booking tickets in advance. This will also allow you to skip the ticket line and go straight to the entrance.

Consider purchasing a Citypass: The Citypass is a multi-attraction pass that offers discounts on admission to a number of top attractions in London, including the Tower of London, St. Paul's Cathedral, and the London Eye. You can purchase the pass online or at participating attractions, and it's valid for 60 days from the date of purchase.

Take breaks: Sightseeing can be tiring, especially if you're on your feet all day. Make sure to take breaks and rest when you need to. You can also consider taking a break for lunch or dinner, as there are plenty of great restaurants and cafes in London.

Wear comfortable shoes: London is a big city, and you'll likely be doing a lot of walking during your sightseeing trip. Make sure to wear comfortable shoes, as you'll be on your feet a lot.

Plan for the weather: London's weather can be unpredictable, so it's important to plan for all eventualities. Make sure to bring a raincoat or umbrella, as well as layers that you can add or remove as needed.

Consider purchasing travel insurance: Travel insurance can provide peace of mind in case of unexpected delays, cancellations, or other unforeseen events. It's a good idea to purchase travel insurance, especially if you're planning a longer trip or if you have a lot of non-refundable expenses.

With these tips, you can create a sightseeing itinerary in London that's tailored to your interests and allows you to make the most of your trip. Whether you're planning a short stay or a longer visit,

London has something for everyone, and with a little planning, you can make the most of your time in this vibrant and exciting city.

How to Purchase Tickets and Discounts for Moving in London
To make the most of your trip, it's important to plan ahead and purchase tickets and discounts in advance. Here are some tips for purchasing tickets and discounts for attractions in London:

Determine which attractions you want to visit: The first step in purchasing tickets and discounts is to decide which attractions you want to visit. Make a list of the landmarks and museums you're interested in, and research their hours of operation, ticket prices, and any special events or exhibits that may be taking place.

Look for discounts and promotions: Many attractions in London offer discounts or promotions for certain groups, such as students, seniors, or families. If you belong to one of these groups, be sure to check if any discounts are available. You can also look for discounts through websites like Groupon or LivingSocial, or by purchasing a Citypass or other multi-attraction pass.

Buy tickets in advance: Many of London's top attractions, such as the Tower of London and the London Eye, can get very busy, especially during peak tourist season. To avoid long lines and ensure that you get a spot, consider buying tickets in advance. You can often purchase tickets online or through a ticket vendor, such as Ticketmaster or See Tickets.

Consider purchasing a travel pass: If you're planning on using public transportation during your trip, consider purchasing a travel pass. London has a number of travel passes available, including the Oyster card and the Visitor Oyster card, which offer discounts on travel on buses, trains, and the Underground. You can purchase these passes at ticket machines or online.

Look for deals and promotions: Keep an eye out for deals and promotions that may be available during your trip. Many attractions offer discounts for booking tickets online or for purchasing tickets in advance, so it pays to plan ahead.

Consider using a tour operator: Tour operators offer a variety of tours and packages that can save you time and money on your trip. Many tour operators offer discounts on admission fees to attractions and other perks, such as transportation and guides. You can find a list of tour operators on the Visit London website.

Check the attraction's website: Many attractions in London offer discounts and promotions directly on their websites. Be sure to check the website of the attraction you're interested in visiting to see if any discounts or promotions are available.

Use a rewards program: If you're a member of a rewards program, such as a hotel loyalty program or a credit card rewards program, you may be able to redeem points or miles for tickets or discounts to attractions in London.

Look for discounts through employee or membership programs: If you're a member of an employee or membership program, such as a union or professional association, you may be able to access discounts on tickets and attractions in London.

Consider purchasing tickets through a third party: There are a number of third-party websites and ticket vendors that offer discounts on tickets to attractions in London. These websites often have a wide selection of tickets available, and you may be able to find discounts or promotions that aren't available elsewhere. Just be sure to check the terms and conditions and compare prices before purchasing tickets through a third party.

CONCLUSION

London is a city with a wide variety of attractions and landmarks to visit, making it the perfect destination for sightseeing. From iconic landmarks such as Buckingham Palace and the Tower Bridge to world-class museums and galleries, there's something for everyone in London.

To make the most of your trip, it's important to plan ahead and purchase tickets and discounts in advance. Look for discounts and promotions, buy tickets online, and consider purchasing a travel pass or tour package to save money and make the most of your time in the city.

CHAPTER 6

SHOPPING IN LONDON

Overview of London's Shopping Scene

London is a shopper's paradise, with a wide variety of shopping options to choose from. From high-end department stores and designer boutiques to colorful markets and independent shops, there's something for everyone in London's shopping scene.

One of the city's most famous shopping destinations is Oxford Street, which is home to a wide variety of high street retailers and department stores, including Selfridges, Debenhams, and John Lewis. The street is also home to the iconic Marble Arch, which marks the beginning of the shopping district.

For luxury brands and designer fashion, head to Knightsbridge and the surrounding area, which is home to iconic stores such as Harrods and Harvey Nichols. You'll also find a number of independent boutiques and designer stores in the neighborhood.

If you're looking for more unique and independent shopping options, head to neighborhoods such as Notting Hill and Camden, which are home to a wide variety of markets, vintage shops, and independent retailers. You'll find everything from antiques and collectibles to handmade jewelry and clothing.

Other popular shopping destinations in London include Covent Garden, which is home to a variety of independent stores and markets, and Westfield, a large shopping center with a wide variety of high street and designer brands.

Moreover, London is home to a number of online retailers and e-commerce sites, making it easy to shop from the comfort of your own home. You can find a wide variety of products, including clothing, accessories, beauty products, and home goods, from a variety of online retailers too.

Tips for Shopping in London

Look for sales and discounts: Many retailers in London offer sales and discounts throughout the year, so it pays to keep an eye out for these deals. You can also sign up for newsletters and follow retailers on social media to stay up-to-date on the latest sales and promotions.

Consider purchasing a shopping pass: London has a number of shopping passes available, which offer discounts on admission fees and other perks, such as discounts at participating retailers. These passes can be a good value if you're planning on doing a lot of shopping during your trip.

Check out markets and independent stores: In addition to traditional retailers, London has a number of markets and independent stores that offer unique and handcrafted items. You can find everything from antiques and collectibles to handmade jewelry and clothing at these stores.

Shop at department stores: London has a number of department stores, including Selfridges, Debenhams, and John Lewis, which offer a wide variety of products, including clothing, accessories, beauty products, and home goods.

Visit high street retailers: The high street is a term used in the UK to refer to main shopping streets in towns and cities. London has a number of high street retailers, including Topshop, Zara, and H&M, which offer a wide selection of clothing and accessories at affordable prices.

Look for designer brands: London is home to a number of designer brands, including Burberry, Alexander McQueen, and Vivienne Westwood. You'll find these brands at department stores and independent boutiques in neighborhoods such as Knightsbridge and Mayfair.

Use cashback and rewards programs: If you're a member of a cashback or rewards program, such as a credit card rewards program or a loyalty program, you may be able to earn points or cashback on your shopping purchases in London.

Take advantage of duty-free shopping: If you're traveling to London from outside the European Union, you may be able to take advantage of duty-free shopping at the airport and some retail stores. Duty-free shopping allows you to purchase items without paying taxes, which can result in significant savings.

Shop online: In addition to traditional bricks-and-mortar stores, London is home to a number of online retailers and e-commerce sites, making it easy to shop from the comfort of your own home. You can find a wide variety of products, including clothing, accessories, beauty products, and home goods, from a variety of online retailers.

Look for secondhand and vintage items: If you're looking for unique and one-of-a-kind items, consider shopping at secondhand and vintage stores in London. You'll find everything from antique furniture and collectibles to vintage clothing and accessories at these stores.

Recommendations for Department Stores, Markets and Specialty Shops

London is a shopper's paradise, with a wide variety of department stores, markets, and specialty shops to choose from. Here are some recommendations for department stores, markets, and specialty shops in London:

Department Stores

Selfridges: This iconic department store is located on Oxford Street and is known for its wide selection of designer brands, fashion, beauty products, and home goods.

Harrods: Located in Knightsbridge, this luxury department store is known for its high-end designer brands, gourmet food hall, and opulent décor.

John Lewis: This department store chain has several locations in London, including on Oxford Street and in the Westfield shopping center. It offers a wide selection of clothing, home goods, and electronics.

Debenhams: This department store chain has several locations in London, including on Oxford Street and in the Westfield shopping center. It offers a wide selection of clothing, beauty products, and home goods.

Marks & Spencer: This department store chain has several locations in London, including on Oxford Street and in the Westfield shopping center. It offers a wide selection of clothing, beauty products, and food.

House of Fraser: This department store chain has several locations in London, including on Oxford Street and in the Westfield shopping center. It offers a wide selection of clothing, beauty products, and home goods.

Markets

Borough Market: Located near London Bridge, this market is known for its fresh produce, artisanal foods, and unique products.

Camden Market: Located in the Camden neighborhood, this market is known for its eclectic mix of clothing, accessories, and souvenirs.

Spitalfields Market: Located in the East End, this market is known for its clothing, accessories, and unique products.

Old Spitalfields Market: Located near Liverpool Street Station, this market is known for its clothing, accessories, and unique products.

Portobello Road Market: Located in the Notting Hill neighborhood, this market is known for its vintage clothing, antiques, and handmade crafts.

Specialty Shops

Notting Hill Market: Located in the Notting Hill neighborhood, this market is known for its vintage clothing, antiques, and handmade crafts.

Hamleys: This toy store, located on Regent Street, is known for its wide selection of toys and games.

The Conran Shop: This specialty store, located in the Marylebone neighborhood, is known for its selection of furniture, home decor, and gifts.

Lush: This cosmetics store, with several locations in London, is known for its handmade and natural beauty products.

The Gardener: This specialty store, located in the Chelsea neighborhood, is known for its selection of gardening supplies and home decor.

The London Map Centre: This specialty store, located in the Covent Garden neighborhood, is known for its selection of maps, globes, and travel guides.

Fortnum & Mason: This high-end food store, located in Piccadilly, is known for its gourmet food and luxury gifts.

Liberty London: This department store, located in the West End, is known for its unique selection of clothing, accessories, and home goods.

The Tate Modern Shop: This specialty shop, located in the Tate Modern museum, is known for its selection of art- and design-related products.

These are just a few recommendations for department stores, markets, and specialty shops in London, but there are many more to choose from. Whether you're looking for luxury brands, unique and independent stores, or fresh produce and artisanal foods, you'll find it in London.

Tips for Finding Good Value and Avoiding Tourists Traps

While there are many great things to see and do in the city, it's important to be aware of tourist traps and overpriced attractions. Here are some tips for finding good value and avoiding tourists traps in London:

❖ **Research before you go**

Before you arrive in London, do some research to find out which attractions and landmarks are worth visiting. Look for reviews from other travelers and consider the cost of admission and any additional fees. This will help you create a budget and ensure that you're getting good value for your money.

❖ **Avoid peak tourist season**

London can get very busy during peak tourist season, which can lead to long lines and overpriced attractions. Consider visiting during the off-season, when crowds are typically smaller and prices may be lower.

❖ Look for discounts and promotions

Many attractions in London offer discounts or promotions for certain groups, such as students, seniors, or families. If you belong to one of these groups, be sure to check if any discounts are available. You can also look for discounts through websites like Groupon or LivingSocial, or by purchasing a Citypass or other multi-attraction pass.

❖ Consider purchasing tickets in advance

Many of London's top attractions, such as the Tower of London and the London Eye, can get very busy, especially during peak tourist season. To avoid long lines and ensure that you get a spot, consider buying tickets in advance. You can often purchase tickets online or through a ticket vendor, such as Ticket Master or See Tickets.

❖ Look for alternative activities

If you're looking to avoid tourist traps and overpriced attractions, consider looking for alternative activities that may be less crowded and more affordable. London has a number of free or low-cost activities, such as visiting parks and gardens, exploring neighborhoods on foot, and attending events and festivals.

❖ Shop around

If you're looking to purchase souvenirs or other items in London, be sure to shop around and compare prices. Don't be afraid to negotiate or haggle for a better price, especially at markets and independent stores.

❖ **Use public transportation**

London has a comprehensive public transportation system, including the Underground (also known as the Tube), buses, and trains. Using public transportation can be a cost-effective and convenient way to get around the city and avoid tourist traps, such as overpriced taxi rides or tour buses.

❖ **Avoid touristy areas**

Many tourist traps are concentrated in areas that are popular with tourists, such as the West End and around major landmarks. Consider exploring less touristy areas of the city, such as neighborhoods like Shoreditch or Brick Lane, which often have a more local feel and may be less expensive.

❖ **Eat like a local**

Instead of eating at restaurants that cater to tourists, consider dining at local pubs, cafes, and restaurants, which often offer good value and a more authentic experience. Look for recommendations from locals or use foodie apps and websites to find the best places to eat.

❖ Stay in a vacation rental or bed and breakfast

Instead of staying at a hotel, consider renting a vacation home or staying at a bed and breakfast, which can often be more affordable and offer a more authentic experience. Websites like Airbnb and HomeAway offer a wide variety of vacation rentals in London, ranging from apartments to entire houses.

CONCLUSION

London is a shopping destination with a wide variety of options to choose from, including high-end department stores, designer boutiques, and colorful markets. To make the most of your shopping trip, it's important to do your research and look for discounts and promotions.

Consider purchasing tickets or passes to save money and time, and look for unique and independent stores for one-of-a-kind items. By following these tips, you'll be able to shop in London like a pro and find the best deals and discounts on a wide variety of products.

CHAPTER 7

ENTERTAINMENT AND NIGHLIFE IN LONDON

Overview of London's Entertainment and Nightlife Scene

London is a vibrant and diverse city, with a wide variety of entertainment and nightlife options to choose from. From live music and theater performances to bars, clubs, and restaurants, there's something for everyone in London's entertainment and nightlife scene.

One of the city's most iconic entertainment venues is the West End, which is home to a number of world-class theaters and musicals. The West End is known for its theater scene, with iconic shows such as "The Lion King," "Les Misérables," and "Wicked" playing at venues such as the London Palladium and the Apollo Victoria Theater.

For live music, London has a number of iconic venues, including the O2 Academy, the Roundhouse, and the Brixton Academy. These venues host a wide variety of acts, from up-and-coming indie bands to international superstars.

In addition to live music and theater, London has a wide variety of bars and clubs to choose from, ranging from trendy rooftop bars to intimate jazz clubs. The city is also home to a number of Michelin-starred restaurants and world-class dining options, making it the perfect place for foodies.

London's nightlife scene is also home to a number of events and festivals, such as the Notting Hill Carnival, which is one of the largest street festivals in Europe, and the London Pride Parade, which celebrates LGBTQ+ culture.

Pub culture: London is known for its pub culture, with a wide variety of traditional pubs to choose from. Many pubs in London serve food and drinks, and some also offer live music or other entertainment. Some iconic pubs in London include the Ye Olde Cheshire Cheese, the Rake, and the Red Lion.

Comedy clubs: London is home to a number of comedy clubs, which host stand-up comedy shows and other comedic performances. Some popular comedy clubs in London include the Comedy Store, the Soho Theatre, and the Glee Club.

Cinemas: London has a number of cinemas, ranging from independent art house theaters to multiplex chains. Many cinemas in London offer special screenings and events, such as movie marathons, themed parties, and advanced screenings of new releases.

Museums and galleries: London has a number of world-class museums and galleries, including the British Museum, the Tate Modern, and the Natural History Museum. Many museums and galleries in London offer special events and exhibitions, as well as late opening hours on certain days.

Outdoor events: London has a number of outdoor events and festivals, such as the Southbank Centre's Festival of Love, the Greenwich and Docklands International Festival, and the London

Literature Festival. These events often feature live music, theater, and other entertainment options.

Karaoke: London has a number of karaoke bars and venues, ranging from traditional Japanese-style karaoke bars to more modern and casual options. Some popular karaoke bars in London include Lucky Voice, AllStar Lanes, and the Camden Head.

Bars and clubs: London has a wide variety of bars and clubs to choose from, ranging from trendy rooftop bars to intimate jazz clubs. Some popular bar and club districts in London include Soho, Shoreditch, and the West End.

Live music: In addition to major music venues, London has a number of smaller live music venues, such as the Lexington and the Jazz Café. These venues host a wide variety of acts, from up-and-coming indie bands to international superstars.

Festivals: London is home to a number of festivals and events throughout the year, including the Notting Hill Carnival, the Greenwich and Docklands International Festival, and the London Literature Festival. These festivals often feature live music, theater, and other entertainment options.

Theater: In addition to the West End, London has a number of other theaters, such as the National Theatre, the Royal Court Theatre, and the Old Vic. These theaters host a wide variety of performances, from classic plays to modern works.

Recommendations for Theaters, Clubs and Live Music Venues
Theaters

The West End: The West End is home to a number of world-class theaters and musicals, such as "The Lion King," "Les Misérables," and "Wicked."

The National Theatre: Located on the South Bank, the National Theatre hosts a variety of performances, including classic plays and modern works.

The Royal Court Theatre: Located in the West End, the Royal Court Theatre is known for its contemporary plays.

The Old Vic: Located in the South Bank, the Old Vic is a historic theater that hosts a variety of performances, including plays and musicals.

The Donmar Warehouse: Located in Covent Garden, the Donmar Warehouse is a small theater that hosts a variety of performances, including plays and musicals.

Clubs

Fabric: Located in Farringdon, Fabric is a popular nightclub that hosts a variety of electronic music events.

Ministry of Sound: Located in Elephant and Castle, Ministry of Sound is a well-known nightclub that hosts a variety of electronic music events.

XOYO: Located in Shoreditch, XOYO is a nightclub that hosts a variety of electronic music events.

The Jazz Café: Located in Camden, the Jazz Café is a live music venue that specializes in jazz, soul, and hip hop music.

The Roundhouse: Located in Camden, the Roundhouse is a live music venue that hosts a variety of concerts and events.

Live music venues

The O2 Academy: Located in various locations around London, the O2 Academy is a live music venue that hosts a variety of concerts and events.

The Brixton Academy: Located in Brixton, the Brixton Academy is a live music venue that hosts a variety of concerts and events.

The Electric Ballroom: Located in Camden, the Electric Ballroom is a live music venue that hosts a variety of concerts and events.

The Lexington: Located in Angel, the Lexington is a live music venue that hosts a variety of concerts and events.

The 100 Club: Located in Oxford Street, the 100 Club is a live music venue that hosts a variety of concerts and events.

The Garage: Located in Highbury, the Garage is a live music venue that hosts a variety of concerts and events.

The Borderline: Located in Soho, the Borderline is a live music venue that hosts a variety of concerts and events.

The Islington Assembly Hall: Located in Islington, the Islington Assembly Hall is a live music venue that hosts a variety of concerts and events.

The Water Rats: Located in King's Cross, the Water Rats is a live music venue that hosts a variety of concerts and events.

The Bush Hall: Located in Shepherd's Bush, the Bush Hall is a live music venue that hosts a variety of concerts and events.

The Moth Club: Located in Hackney, the Moth Club is a live music venue that hosts a variety of concerts and events.

The Dome: Located in Tufnell Park, the Dome is a live music venue that hosts a variety of concerts and events.

The Half Moon: Located in Putney, the Half Moon is a live music venue that hosts a variety of concerts and events.

The O2 Forum: Located in Kentish Town, the O2 Forum is a live music venue that hosts a variety of concerts and events.

The O2 Shepherds Bush Empire: Located in Shepherd's Bush, the O2 Shepherds Bush Empire is a live music venue that hosts a variety of concerts and events.

The O2 Academy Islington: Located in Islington, the O2 Academy Islington is a live music venue that hosts a variety of concerts and events.

The O2 Academy Brixton: Located in Brixton, the O2 Academy Brixton is a live music venue that hosts a variety of concerts and events.

The O2 Academy Birmingham: Located in Birmingham, the O2 Academy Birmingham is a live music venue that hosts a variety of concerts and events.

The O2 Academy Glasgow: Located in Glasgow, the O2 Academy Glasgow is a live music venue that hosts a variety of concerts and events.

The O2 Academy Liverpool: Located in Liverpool, the O2 Academy Liverpool is a live music venue that hosts a variety of concerts and events.

Tips for Finding Good Value and Staying Safe in London

London is a vibrant and diverse city with a lot to offer, but it's important to stay safe and be aware of your surroundings when visiting. Here are some tips for finding good value and staying safe in London:

Research before you go: Before you arrive in London, do some research to find out which attractions and landmarks are worth visiting, as well as the best areas to stay in and what to expect from the local culture. This will help you plan your trip and ensure that you have a safe and enjoyable experience.

Use public transportation: London has a comprehensive public transportation system, including the Underground (also known as the Tube), buses, and trains. Using public transportation can be a cost-effective and convenient way to get around the city and avoid tourist traps, such as overpriced taxi rides or tour buses.

Be aware of your surroundings: London is a busy city, and it's important to be aware of your surroundings at all times. Keep an eye on your belongings and stay alert when walking around, especially at night. Avoid walking alone in deserted areas, and be aware of your surroundings when using public transportation.

Know where to find help: If you need help or assistance while in London, know where to go for help. Police stations, hospitals, and embassies are all good places to go for assistance.

Use common sense: As with any city, it's important to use common sense when traveling in London. Avoid displaying expensive items, such as jewelry or electronics, and be mindful of your personal safety. If something doesn't feel right, trust your instincts and take steps to protect yourself.

Look for discounts: There are many ways to save money in London, such as purchasing tickets or passes for attractions and landmarks, looking for discounts on accommodation, and eating at local restaurants. Websites like Groupon and Time Out often have discounts and promotions on events and activities in London.

Use a travel app: There are many travel apps that can help you save money and stay safe in London. Apps like Citymapper and Google Maps can help you navigate the city, while apps like XE Currency can help you find the best exchange rates and budget your trip.

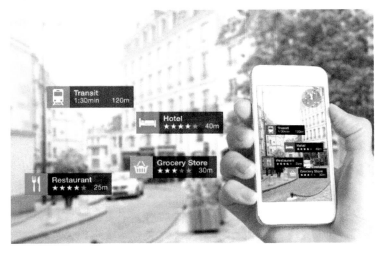

Avoid tourist traps: Many tourist traps are concentrated in areas that are popular with tourists, such as the West End and around major landmarks. Consider exploring less touristy areas of the city, such as neighborhoods like Shoreditch or Brick Lane, which often have a more local feel and may be less expensive.

Stay in a vacation rental or bed and breakfast: Instead of staying at a hotel, consider renting a vacation home or staying at a bed and breakfast, which can often be more affordable and offer a more authentic experience. Websites like Airbnb and HomeAway offer a wide variety of vacation rentals in London, ranging from apartments to entire houses.

Get travel insurance: It's always a good idea to get travel insurance before you go on a trip, especially to a city like London where you may be more exposed to risks like theft or accidents. Travel insurance can provide peace of mind and help protect you in case of any unforeseen events.

CONCLUSION

Overall, London's entertainment and nightlife scene is diverse, vibrant, and always evolving, offering something for everyone. Whether you're interested in live music, theater, or dining and drinking, you'll find it in London.

CHAPTER 8

DAY TRIPS FROM LONDON

Overview of Popular Day Trips From London

London is a great city to visit, but it's also a great base for exploring the surrounding area. Here is an overview of some popular day trips from London:

❖ **Stonehenge**

Located about 90 minutes west of London, Stonehenge is a prehistoric monument that is a UNESCO World Heritage site. Visitors can walk around the monument and learn about its history and significance.

❖ **Oxford**

Located about an hour northwest of London, Oxford is a historic university town that is home to the University of Oxford, one of the oldest and most prestigious universities in the world. Visitors can tour the university's colleges, visit the Ashmolean Museum, and explore the town's charming streets.

❖ Cambridge

Located about an hour northeast of London, Cambridge is another historic university town that is home to the University of Cambridge, another prestigious university. Visitors can tour the university's colleges, visit the Fitzwilliam Museum, and explore the town's charming streets.

❖ Bath

Located about 90 minutes west of London, Bath is a historic city that is home to the Roman Baths, a well-preserved Roman spa that is a UNESCO World Heritage site. Visitors can tour the baths, visit the Fashion Museum, and explore the city's charming streets.

❖ Stratford-upon-Avon

Located about two hours northwest of London, Stratford-upon-Avon is the birthplace of William Shakespeare and is home to a number of historic sites related to the famous playwright. Visitors can tour the Shakespeare Birthplace Trust, visit the Royal Shakespeare Company, and explore the city's charming streets.

❖ Greenwich

Located about 20 minutes east of London, Greenwich is a historic town that is home to the Royal Observatory, which is the home of the Prime Meridian line, and the Cutty Sark, a 19th-century sailing ship. Visitors can tour these landmarks, visit the National Maritime Museum, and explore the town's charming streets.

❖ Winchester

Located about an hour southwest of London, Winchester is a historic city that is home to Winchester Cathedral, a UNESCO World Heritage site, and Winchester Castle. Visitors can tour these landmarks, visit the Winchester City Mill, and explore the city's charming streets.

❖ Leeds Castle

Located about an hour southeast of London, Leeds Castle is a historic castle that is surrounded by beautiful gardens and parkland. Visitors can tour the castle, visit the aviary, and explore the grounds.

❖ Dover

Located about an hour and a half southeast of London, Dover is a coastal town that is home to the iconic White Cliffs of Dover and Dover Castle, a well-preserved medieval castle that is a UNESCO World Heritage site. Visitors can tour the castle, visit the Dover Museum, and explore the town's charming streets.

❖ Canterbury

Located about an hour southeast of London, Canterbury is a historic city that is home to Canterbury Cathedral, a UNESCO World Heritage site, and the Canterbury Tales Museum. Visitors can tour the cathedral, visit the museum, and explore the city's charming streets.

❖ Royal Tunbridge Wells

Located about an hour southeast of London, Royal Tunbridge Wells is a charming spa town that is home to the Tunbridge Wells Museum and Art Gallery and the Pantiles, a historic shopping and dining area. Visitors can tour the museum, explore the Pantiles, and visit the town's many parks and gardens.

❖ Windsor

Located about an hour west of London, Windsor is a historic town that is home to Windsor Castle, a well-preserved medieval castle that is the residence of Queen Elizabeth II. Visitors can tour the castle, visit the Windsor Great Park, and explore the town's charming streets.

❖ Kew Gardens

Located about 20 minutes southwest of London, Kew Gardens is a botanical garden that is home to a variety of plants and flowers from around the world. Visitors can tour the gardens, visit the Kew Palace, and explore the many trails and paths.

❖ The Cotswolds

Located about two hours west of London, the Cotswolds is a picturesque region of rolling hills and charming villages that is popular with tourists. Visitors can explore the charming villages, visit historic sites such as the ancient Neolithic monument at Avebury, and enjoy the beautiful countryside.

❖ Brighton

Located about an hour south of London, Brighton is a popular seaside town that is known for its pier, beaches, and vibrant arts and culture scene. Visitors can walk along the pier, visit the Royal Pavilion, and explore the city's many museums, galleries, and shops.

❖ The New Forest

Located about an hour and a half southwest of London, the New Forest is a beautiful area of woodland, heathland, and countryside that is home to a variety of wildlife. Visitors can explore the forest, visit the New Forest Wildlife Park, and enjoy the many walking and cycling trails.

❖ Salisbury

Located about an hour and a half southwest of London, Salisbury is a historic city that is home to Salisbury Cathedral, a well-preserved medieval cathedral that is a UNESCO World Heritage site. Visitors can tour the cathedral, visit the Salisbury Museum, and explore the city's charming streets.

❖ Southampton

Located about an hour and a half southwest of London, Southampton is a city on the south coast of England that is home to the SeaCity Museum and the Southampton Maritime Museum. Visitors can tour the museums, visit the Southampton Waterfront, and explore the city's many parks and gardens.

❖ The South Downs

Located about an hour and a half south of London, the South Downs is a beautiful area of rolling hills and countryside that is home to a variety of wildlife. Visitors can explore the countryside, visit the South Downs National Park Visitor Centre, and enjoy the many walking and cycling trails.

❖ The Thames Path

Located along the river Thames, the Thames Path is a long-distance walking and cycling trail that runs through London and the surrounding area. Visitors can explore the trail, visit the many towns and villages along the way, and enjoy the beautiful countryside.

Tips for Planning a Day Trip to London
Choose your destination: There are so many interesting places to visit in and around London, so it's important to choose a destination that aligns with your interests and budget. Do some research and make a list of the places you'd like to visit, and then narrow it down to the ones that are most feasible for a day trip.

Plan your transportation: London is easily accessible by public transportation, so consider taking the train or bus to your destination. The National Rail website and the National Express website both offer a range of options for travel within the UK. You can also consider driving, but be aware that traffic can be heavy and parking can be expensive in London.

Book tickets and accommodations in advance: If you're planning to visit a specific attraction or event, it's a good idea to book tickets and accommodations in advance to avoid disappointment. Websites like VisitBritain and Time Out offer a range of options for tickets and accommodations, as well as special offers and discounts.

Pack wisely: London can be unpredictable weather-wise, so it's a good idea to pack layers and a raincoat. Don't forget to bring your camera, a map, and any other essentials you might need for your trip.

Stay safe: As with any city, it's important to be aware of your surroundings and take precautions to stay safe. Avoid walking alone in deserted areas, and be aware of your belongings when using public transportation.

Start early: London is a busy city, so it's a good idea to start your day early to avoid crowds and traffic. This will also give you more time to explore and enjoy your destination.

Take breaks: London can be a hectic city, so it's important to take breaks and rest when you need to. Consider finding a park or green space to relax in, or taking a break at a café or restaurant.

Be flexible: It's always a good idea to be flexible when traveling, as things don't always go according to plan. If you're unable to visit a particular attraction or event, or if the weather isn't cooperating, don't be afraid to pivot and try something else.

Use public transportation: London has a comprehensive public transportation system, including the Underground (also known as the Tube), buses, and trains. Using public transportation can be a convenient and cost-effective way to get around the city and avoid traffic.

Stay hydrated: London can be warm and humid in the summer, so it's important to stay hydrated. Make sure to bring a bottle of water with you and drink it regularly throughout the day.

Consider a tour: If you're short on time or would like to make the most of your day trip to London, you might want to consider taking a tour. There are many companies that offer guided tours of London, ranging from walking tours to bus tours to boat tours.

Try local food: London is known for its diverse cuisine, so make sure to try some local food while you're in the city. From fish and chips to curry to pub grub, there's something for everyone.

Take a break from the city: If you're looking for a break from the hustle and bustle of the city, consider taking a day trip to one of London's beautiful parks or gardens. The Royal Parks, such as Hyde Park and Kensington Gardens, offer a range of activities and attractions, including walking and cycling trails, playgrounds, and picnic areas.

Don't overdo it: It's important to pace yourself when planning a day trip to London, as there is so much to see and do. Don't try to fit too much into one day, as you'll likely be tired and overwhelmed. Instead, focus on a few key activities or attractions and take your time to enjoy them.

How to Get to London from Anywhere in the World

London is a major global city and is easily accessible from anywhere in the world. Here are some tips on how to get to London from various locations around the world:

From the United States

By air: There are many direct flights from major cities in the United States to London, with multiple airlines offering service. The cost of a round-trip ticket from New York to London, for example, can range from $400 to $1,500 or more, depending on the time of year and how far in advance you book.

By train: While it's not possible to travel to London by train from the United States, you can take the Eurostar train from Paris or Brussels to London. The cost of a one-way ticket from Paris to London starts at around €35, while the cost of a one-way ticket from Brussels to London starts at around €40.

From Europe

By air: There are many direct flights from major cities in Europe to London, with multiple airlines offering service. The cost of a round-trip ticket from Paris to London, for example, can range from €50 to €200 or more, depending on the time of year and how far in advance you book.

By train: The Eurostar train offers service from several cities in Europe to London, including Paris, Brussels, Amsterdam, and

Rotterdam. The cost of a one-way ticket from Paris to London starts at around €35, while the cost of a one-way ticket from Brussels to London starts at around €40.

From Canada

By air: There are many direct flights from major cities in Canada to London, with multiple airlines offering service. The cost of a round-trip ticket from Toronto to London, for example, can range from CAD 500 to CAD 2,000 or more, depending on the time of year and how far in advance you book.

From Africa

By air: There are many direct flights from major cities in Africa to London, with multiple airlines offering service. The cost of a round-trip ticket from Johannesburg to London, for example, can range from ZAR 8,000 to ZAR 20,000 or more, depending on the time of year and how far in advance you book.

From Asia

By air: There are many direct flights from major cities in Asia to London, with multiple airlines offering service. The cost of a round-trip ticket from Tokyo to London, for example, can range from JPY 80,000 to JPY 200,000 or more, depending on the time of year and how far in advance you book.

From Australia

By air: There are many direct flights from major cities in Australia to London, with multiple airlines offering service. The cost of a round-trip ticket from Sydney to London, for example, can range from AUD 1,500 to AUD 4,000 or more, depending on the time of year and how far in advance you book.

Keep in mind that these are just estimates, and the actual cost of a trip to London from these locations may vary depending on a range of factors. It's always a good idea to compare prices and book as far in advance as possible to get the best deal.

Recommendations for Destinations Based on Interests
For history buffs

The British Museum: This world-famous museum is home to a range of historical artifacts from around the world, including the Rosetta Stone and the Elgin Marbles.

The Tower of London: This historic castle is home to the Crown Jewels and offers guided tours of its many chambers and dungeons.

Buckingham Palace: The official residence of the British monarchy, Buckingham Palace is a must-see for history buffs. Visitors can watch the Changing of the Guard ceremony, which takes place daily at 11:30 a.m.

For art lovers

The Tate Modern: This contemporary art museum is home to a range of modern and contemporary art, including works by artists such as Warhol, Picasso, and Hockney.

The National Gallery: Located in the heart of London, this museum is home to a range of European paintings from the 13th to the 19th centuries, including works by artists such as Da Vinci, Rembrandt, and Monet.

The Saatchi Gallery: This contemporary art gallery is home to a range of modern and contemporary art, including works by emerging and established artists.

For nature lovers

The Royal Botanic Gardens, Kew: Located in southwest London, these gardens are home to a range of plants and flowers from around the world, as well as a variety of wildlife.

Hampstead Heath: This large park in north London is home to a range of walking and cycling trails, as well as a variety of wildlife.

The London Wetland Centre: Located in southwest London, this nature reserve is home to a range of wetland animals and plants, as well as a variety of walking and cycling trails.

For foodies

Borough Market: This popular food market is located in south London and is home to a variety of stalls selling fresh produce, bread, cheese, and other specialty foods.

Camden Market: This popular market is located in north London and is home to a variety of stalls selling street food, clothing, and other goods.

Brick Lane: This street in east London is known for its vibrant food scene, with a range of restaurants, cafes, and food stalls serving a variety of cuisines.

For shopping enthusiasts

Oxford Street: This popular shopping street is home to a range of high street and department stores, as well as a variety of independent shops.

Camden Market: In addition to its food stalls, Camden Market is also home to a variety of clothing, jewelry, and other goods.

Covent Garden: This popular shopping and entertainment district is home to a range of high street and independent shops, as well as a variety of restaurants and bars.

For theater and performing arts enthusiasts

The West End: The West End is London's theater district and is home to a range of theaters, including the Lyceum Theatre, the Palace Theatre, and the Apollo Theatre.

The Royal Opera House: Located in Covent Garden, the Royal Opera House is home to the Royal Opera and the Royal Ballet.

The Barbican Centre: This arts and entertainment complex is home to a range of performing arts, including theater, music, and dance.

For sports fans

Wembley Stadium: This iconic stadium is home to the England national football team and hosts a range of sporting events, including football, rugby, and concerts.

Twickenham Stadium: This stadium is home to the England national rugby team and hosts a range of rugby and other sporting events.

The All England Lawn Tennis Club: Located in southwest London, this club is home to the Wimbledon Lawn Tennis Championships, which take place annually in June and July.

CONCLUSION

London is a city that has a lot to offer, but it's also surrounded by many interesting and beautiful places that make for great day trips. Whether you're interested in history, nature, or just want to get out of the city for a while, there are plenty of options to choose from.

Some popular destinations include Stonehenge, Bath, and Oxford, but there are many other charming towns and villages just a short train or car ride away. No matter what you're looking for, there's sure to be a day trip from London that will suit your interests and preferences.

So if you're visiting London and want to see more of the surrounding area, don't hesitate to make some plans and get out of the city for a while.

CHAPTER 9

PLANNING YOUR TRIP TO LONDON

Tips for Budgeting and Planning

  ❖ **Research and compare flight prices**

When it comes to budgeting for your trip to London, one of the biggest expenses will likely be the cost of flights. To get the best deal, it's important to do your research and compare prices from different airlines and online travel agencies. Don't forget to also consider the cost of additional fees, such as baggage and seat selection.

  ❖ **Look for discounts and promotions**

There are many ways to save money on your trip to London, and one of the best is to take advantage of discounts and promotions. This could include things like early bird discounts on flights or hotels, group rates, and special deals for students or military personnel. Be sure to keep an eye out for these offers, as they can help you save a significant amount of money.

  ❖ **Consider staying in a budget hotel or hostel**

Accommodation is another big expense when traveling, and it's important to find a place to stay that fits your budget. If you're looking to save money, consider staying in a budget hotel or hostel instead of a more expensive luxury hotel. These options may not be as fancy, but they can still provide you with a comfortable place to sleep and a chance to experience local culture.

  ❖ **Use public transportation**

London has an extensive public transportation system that includes buses, trains, and the underground (known as the

"Tube"). These options can be more cost-effective than taking taxis or renting a car, especially if you're planning to visit multiple destinations in the city. Be sure to purchase an Oyster card, which allows you to pay for your trips on the Tube, buses, and other forms of public transportation with a single card.

❖ **Purchase a city pass**

If you're planning to visit multiple attractions in London, you might consider purchasing a city pass. These passes allow you to visit multiple attractions for a discounted price and can save you a significant amount of money over the course of your trip. There are several different city passes available, so be sure to research and compare the options to find the one that best fits your needs.

❖ **Use discount codes and vouchers**

Many attractions in London offer discounts or vouchers that can be used to save money on admission. Be sure to look for these discounts and vouchers before you visit an attraction, as they can help you save a considerable amount of money. You can often find these discounts online, through local tourism offices, or at the attraction itself.

❖ **Eat like a local**

Dining out in London can be expensive, especially if you're eating at more upscale restaurants. To save money, consider eating like a local and trying some of the city's more affordable dining options. This could include things like street food, markets, and local pubs. Not only will these options be more budget-friendly, but they'll also give you a chance to experience local culture and cuisine.

❖ **Use coupons and vouchers for dining**

In addition to eating at more affordable dining options, you can also save money on your meals by using coupons and vouchers. These discounts are often available through local tourism offices or online, and they can be used at a variety of restaurants and cafes throughout the city.

❖ **Use a travel credit card**

If you have a travel credit card, you might be able to save money on your trip to London by using it to make purchases. Many travel credit cards offer rewards and points that can be redeemed for travel-related expenses, such as flights, hotels, and more. Be sure to research the different options and find a card that fits your needs and budget.

❖ Consider staying in an Airbnb

If you're looking for a more budget-friendly accommodation option, you might consider staying in an Airbnb. These rental properties are often more affordable than traditional hotels and can offer a unique and authentic experience. Just be sure to read reviews and communicate with the host before booking to ensure that the property meets your needs and expectations.

❖ Use a travel rewards program

Many airlines and hotels offer travel rewards programs that allow you to earn points or miles for your trips. These points can then be redeemed for flights, hotels, or other travel-related expenses. By using a travel rewards program, you'll be able to save money on your trip to London and potentially earn other perks and benefits.

❖ Use cash or a debit card instead of a credit card

While it's always a good idea to have a credit card for emergencies, you might want to consider using cash or a debit card for everyday expenses during your trip to London. This can help you better manage your budget and avoid overspending.

❖ Avoid peak tourist season

The cost of flights and accommodation in London tends to be higher during peak tourist season, which is typically from June to August. If you're willing to travel during the off-season, you'll likely be able to find better deals and save money on your trip.

❖ Avoid tourist traps

While it might be tempting to visit all the popular tourist attractions in London, these can often be expensive and crowded. To save money, consider visiting some of the city's lesser-known destinations or opting for free activities instead.

❖ **Walk or bike instead of taking taxis or public transportation**

If you're staying in a central location, you might be able to save money on transportation by walking or biking instead of taking taxis or public transportation. Not only will this save you money, but it will also allow you to experience the city in a more authentic and immersive way.

❖ **Pack light**

By packing light, you'll be able to save money on baggage fees and avoid the hassle of lugging around heavy bags. This will also make it easier to get around the city, as you won't have to worry about carrying a lot of stuff with you.

❖ **Use apps to find the best deals**

There are many apps available that can help you find the best deals on flights, accommodation, and activities in London. By using these apps, you'll be able to save money and make the most of your trip.

❖ **Don't be afraid to negotiate**

In many cases, it's possible to negotiate a better deal on flights, accommodation, and other travel-related expenses. If you're flexible and willing to negotiate, you might be able to save money on your trip to London.

❖ **Consider staying in a vacation rental or house swap**

If you're traveling with a group or want more space, you might consider staying in a vacation rental or participating in a house swap. These options can often be more affordable than traditional hotels and can provide a unique and authentic experience.

❖ **Shop around for travel insurance**

Travel insurance can help protect you in case of unexpected events, such as flight cancellations or medical emergencies. However, it's important to shop around and compare different insurance policies to find the one that best fits your needs and budget.

❖ **Make use of free activities**

London has a lot of free activities to enjoy, including parks, museums, and cultural events. By taking advantage of these free activities, you'll be able to save money and still have a great time.

❖ **Consider purchasing a travel package**

Travel packages can sometimes offer discounts on flights, accommodation, and activities, and can be a convenient way to plan your trip to London. Just be sure to compare prices and read the fine print to ensure that you're getting a good deal.

❖ **Look for discounts for students and military personnel**

If you're a student or military personnel, you might be able to take advantage of discounts on flights, accommodation, and activities in London. Be sure to bring your ID or other proof of eligibility to take advantage of these discounts.

❖ **Consider a self-guided tour**

Self-guided tours can be a cost-effective way to explore London, as you'll be able to go at your own pace and customize your itinerary. You can often find self-guided tour options for a variety of destinations and interests, such as food, history, and art.

❖ **Use a budget planner**

A budget planner can be a helpful tool for planning your trip to London and staying on track with your budget. You can use a budget planner to track your expenses, set budget goals, and identify areas where you can save money.

❖ **Use a rewards program for car rentals**

Many car rental companies offer rewards programs that allow you to earn points or discounts on future rentals. If you're planning to rent a car during your trip to London, be sure to look for a rewards program that fits your needs.

❖ **Consider a guided tour**

While guided tours can be more expensive than self-guided options, they can also be a convenient and hassle-free way to explore London. Guided tours often include transportation, admission to attractions, and the services of a knowledgeable guide, which can make them a good value for the money.

❖ **Don't be afraid to ask for help**

If you're having trouble budgeting and planning your trip to London, don't be afraid to ask for help. You can ask for advice from friends and family, seek the guidance of a travel agent, or consult with a financial planner. With the right help and resources, you'll be able to plan a budget-friendly trip to London that meets your needs and goals.

Information on Visas and Travel Insurance
Visa

If you're planning to visit London, you'll need to determine whether you need a visa and, if so, how to obtain one. The requirements for a visa will depend on your country of citizenship, the purpose of your visit, and the length of your stay.

Generally, citizens of countries in the European Economic Area (EEA) and Switzerland do not need a visa to enter the UK for stays of up to 6 months. Citizens of certain other countries, such as the United States and Canada, may also be able to enter the UK without a visa for short stays.

If you do need a visa, you'll need to apply for one through the UK Visa and Immigration website or at a UK embassy or consulate in your country of residence. You'll typically need to complete an application and provide supporting documents, such as a passport, photos, and proof of financial stability. You may also need to pay a fee and attend an interview at the embassy or consulate.

It's important to start the visa process as early as possible, as it can take several weeks or even months to obtain a visa. Be sure to check the visa requirements for your country and the specific type of visa you need, as these can vary.

Travel Insurance

Travel insurance is a type of insurance that covers unexpected events and expenses that may occur during a trip. This could include things like flight cancellations, medical emergencies, lost luggage, and more.

If you're planning to visit London, it's a good idea to consider purchasing travel insurance to protect yourself in case of any unexpected events. There are many different types of travel insurance available, and the coverage will depend on the policy you choose.

Some common types of coverage offered by travel insurance policies include trip cancellation coverage, medical coverage, and emergency evacuation coverage. You may also be able to add on additional coverage for things like rental car accidents, adventure sports, and natural disasters.

To purchase travel insurance, you'll typically need to provide information about your trip, including the dates, destinations, and activities you'll be participating in. You may also need to answer questions about your health and provide proof of any pre-existing medical conditions.

When shopping for travel insurance, it's important to compare policies and read the fine print to ensure that you're getting the coverage you need. Be sure to also check whether your existing insurance coverage, such as health insurance or credit card insurance, offers any protection for your trip.

It's worth noting that the UK has a universal healthcare system called the National Health Service (NHS), which provides free or low-cost medical treatment to residents and visitors. However, the NHS does not cover things like emergency evacuation or lost luggage, so it's still a good idea to consider purchasing travel insurance.

In summary, if you're planning to visit London, you'll need to determine whether you need a visa and, if so, how to obtain one. It's also a good idea to consider purchasing travel insurance to protect yourself in case of any unexpected events. By researching and understanding the requirements and options available to you, you'll be better prepared for your trip to London.

Recommendations for Resources and Tools for your Travel to London (Travel Guides, Maps, Apps etc.)

When planning your trip to London, there are a number of resources and tools that can help you make the most of your trip. Some recommendations include:

Travel guides

Travel guides are a useful resource for anyone planning a trip to London, as they provide information on the city's top attractions, restaurants, and other points of interest. There are many different travel guides available, both in book form and online.

For example, the Lonely Planet London travel guide is a popular book that provides detailed information on the city, including maps, recommendations for things to see and do, and practical tips for getting around. Online resources like Tripadvisor also offer a wealth of information on London, including user reviews and ratings of hotels, restaurants, and attractions.

Maps

Maps are an essential tool for any trip, and London is no exception. You can use a physical map, such as a city map or a London Underground map, to help you navigate the city and plan your itinerary. Alternatively, you can use an online mapping tool like Google Maps to find your way around London. Google Maps provides real-time traffic updates, public transportation information, and the ability to search for points of interest and get directions.

Apps

There are many apps available that can help you plan and make the most of your trip to London. Some useful apps include:

Citymapper: This app provides real-time public transportation information and helps you plan your route around the city. You can search for the best route by bus, train, or bike, and the app will provide updates on delays and disruptions.

Time Out London: This app provides information on events, restaurants, and other points of interest in London, as well as personalized recommendations based on your interests. You can search for things to do by category, location, or date, and the app will provide details on ticket prices, schedules, and other information.

The London Pass: This app allows you to purchase and use a city pass, which provides discounted admission to many of London's top attractions. The app includes a digital guidebook with information on participating attractions, and you can use the pass to skip the line at many popular sites.

Travel forums

Travel forums are a great way to get advice and recommendations from other travelers who have visited London. You can find forums on websites like Tripadvisor or Lonely Planet, where you can ask questions and get tips from people who have recently visited the city. For example, you might ask for recommendations on the best neighborhoods to stay in, or advice on how to save money on your trip.

Local tourism offices

Local tourism offices can be a great resource for planning your trip to London, as they can provide information on attractions, events, and other points of interest in the city. You can often find tourism offices online or in person, and they can often provide brochures, maps, and other helpful materials. For example, you might visit the Visit London website or stop by the London & Partners Visitor Centre to get information on things to do in the city.

CONCLUSION

Planning your trip to London requires careful consideration of a number of factors, including your budget, accommodation, transportation, and activities. By using resources and tools like travel guides, maps, apps, travel forums, and local tourism offices, you'll be able to plan a trip that meets your needs and goals.

It's also important to research visa requirements and consider purchasing travel insurance to protect yourself in case of any unexpected events. By taking the time to plan carefully, you'll be able to make the most of your trip to London and have a memorable and enjoyable experience.

Printed in Great Britain
by Amazon

17795789R00071